Karen Blixen (Dinesen was her maiden name and Isak her *nom de plume*) arrived in Kenya in 1914 to start a new life with her Swedish cousin, Baron Bror Blixen. In time she grew to love the land and its people, to count on her faithful Somali servant, Farah, and on the friendship of two maverick pioneers, Berkeley Cole and Denys Finch Hatton. The bankruptcy of her farm, a failed marriage, and a series of personal tragedies eventually drove her from Kenya and left her life in shreds. In later years, however, her memories became the source of one of the most beautiful books ever written, *Out of Africa*. To write the screenplay, Kurt Luedtke drew not only on this memorable Dinesen book, but on her subsequent works, *Shadows on the Grass* and *Letters From Africa*, as well as on biographies of Dinesen and Denys Finch Hatton, *Isak Dinesen: The Life of a Storyteller* by Judith Thurman and *Silence Will Speak* by Errol Trzebinski. Read as a script, the *Out of Africa* screenplay captures the unique rhythm of Dinesen's love story—a piece of writing, says director Sydney Pollack, "to be enjoyed in and of itself." But it also provides insights into how a director, screenwriter, and others collaborated to transform literature and biography into a remarkable film.

"*Out of Africa* provides old-movie lushness and romance without ever underestimating its characters', or the audience's, intelligence. It's a splendid journey, with a first-class ticket."
— David Ansen, *Newsweek*

"One of the most thoroughly absorbing movies I have seen in a very long time."
— Julie Salmon, *Wall Street Journal*

"Now across a vast span of time and distance, a movie director, working artfully in his own medium, has answered Dinesen's spirit and amplified it. . . . *Out of Africa* is, at last, the free-spirited, fullhearted gesture that everyone has been waiting for the movies to make all decade long. It reclaims the emotional territory that is rightfully theirs."
— Richard Schickel, *Time*

OUT OF AFRICA

THE SHOOTING SCRIPT

SCREENPLAY BY
KURT LUEDTKE

INTRODUCED AND
ANNOTATED BY
SYDNEY POLLACK

NEWMARKET PRESS
New York

87 88 89 90 91 MPC 10 9 8 7 6 5 4 3 2 1   hc

87 88 89 90 91 MPC 10 9 8 7 6 5 4 3 2 1   pbk

Library of Congress Cataloging-in-Publication Data

Luedtke, Kurt.
  Out of Africa.

  1. Dinesen, Isak, 1885–1962, in fiction, drama, poetry,
etc.   I. Pollack, Sydney, 1934–   II. Title.
PN1997.087   1987   791.43'72   86-61993
ISBN 0-937858-85-4
ISBN 0-937858-84-6 (pbk.)

Quantity Purchases
Companies, professional groups, clubs, and other organizations may qualify for special terms when ordering quantities of this title.
For information, contact the Special Sales Department, Newmarket Press, 18 East 48th Street, New York, New York 10017, (212) 832-3575.

Book design by Anne Scatto/Levavi & Levavi

Manufactured in the United States of America

CONTENTS

Director Sydney Pollack (above) on the set during the filming of *Out of Africa* and screenwriter Kurt Luedtke (right). PHOTOS BY FRANK CONNOR.

INTRODUCTION

This wasn't the first time an attempt had been made to film Isak Dinesen's *Out of Africa*. It was, however, the first time it had been attempted by screenwriter Kurt Luedtke. It was also the first time a screenwriter and filmmaker had Judith Thurman's extraordinary biography, *Isak Dinesen: The Life of a Storyteller*, to work with. It was Kurt's perceptions and grasp of the material and Judith's insights that enabled us to make the film of Karen Blixen's years in Africa.

In 1979, Kurt, a former newspaperman from Detroit, brought me an original screenplay called *Absence of Malice*. Although it was his first attempt at screenwriting, it was fascinating and rich material, powerfully written and full of invention. We made the film and Kurt was nominated for an Academy Award. It wasn't beginner's luck. He is an extraordinary writer—an excellent constructionist and an excellent scene writer. That's a rare combination. He's also smart, a tireless worker, and he writes about things that matter to him.

Everyone who makes a film thinks his film was difficult. More difficult than most. I'm no different. I think *Out of Africa* was difficult. More difficult than most. The central problem we faced in bringing Dinesen's book to the screen was its lack of conventional narrative. A pastorale, a beautifully formed memoir that relies on Dinesen's prose style, her sense of poetry, and her ability to discover large truths in very small, specific details, *Out of Africa* is deeply affecting but very elusive material on which to base a screenplay. As is often the case with fine writing, her marvelous prose is deceptive. The fact that the work is anecdotal and virtually without a narrative spine is easy to miss. There is about *Out of Africa* a seductive sense of great loss from which it is possible to infer that somehow a tragedy has occurred, that a story for a film is somewhere to be found among her guarded memories. What is beguiling about *Out of Africa* is not that which has been told, but that which has remained deliberately untold. If you enjoyed the film or are touched by what you read here, it is because Kurt's screenplay succeeds in giving the material a narrative shape and in capturing the rhythm and intentions of Dinesen's prose:

This is either the sixth or seventh draft; we have all lost track. The screenplay was worked on continually, from the first draft (completed in December of 1982) through the final shooting day, June 6, 1985. Kurt did the first draft alone, then he and I spent most of 1983 doing two more drafts. Nineteen eighty-four was a preparation and pre-production year, and our friend David Rayfiel helped us through three or four more drafts. Kurt and David sometimes worked alone, sometimes together, and then the three of us would meet and push through the script from the beginning. After shooting finally started, I spent several hours a week on the phone from Africa, working on the final polish with Kurt and David. I had the additional benefit of having Judith Thurman looking over my shoulder in Africa as our technical advisor.

What's published here is our shooting script; however, since the writing process continues on into the shooting and the editing, there were sometimes rearrangements in addition to simple deletions. Often these rearrangements were quite complicated. For this reason I've tried to indicate at various points where the finished film deviates from this final shooting script. For those interested in film construction it seems to me worth the effort to unscramble and compare the two versions.

One of the most substantive changes we made in the rewriting process was the film's opening—the notion of beginning as though Karen is going back in time to reexamine Denys, and perhaps clarify him finally for herself: "I've written about all the others, not because I loved them less, but because they were clearer . . . easier." This opening montage was intended to suggest memory, establish a rhythm and pace, and dictate a kind of style.

Throughout the rewrite we struggled with the character of Denys Finch Hatton, an elusive man living at emotional distance from those around him. How were we to dramatize this lack of involvement? During one of our work sessions we were discussing a sequence in which Denys (already living with Karen in this version) learns that his best friend, Berkeley, who is having a love affair with a Somali woman, is about to die. Someone said, "What if Denys doesn't know about his best friend's girlfriend? Isn't that emotional distance?" So we reconstructed the scene to show Denys discovering the love affair for the first time. Completely bewildered, he asks the man he thinks of as his best friend: "Why didn't you tell me?" To which Berkeley replies: "I suppose . . . I think I didn't know you well enough." Then by placing this new scene *before* the scene in which Denys asks to move in with Karen, we felt three things were accomplished: first, an instance was found in which to dramatize Denys's emotional elusiveness; second, a real motivation or need was created for his moving in with Karen, and finally, Denys's realization of how Berkeley thought about him created a change, a new way of looking at himself, a development, in character terms.

To begin in Denmark or not to begin in Denmark? The question came up almost every work session. Was it necessary to see Karen there before she discovered Africa? Would the contrast between that small, snowy country, her life there, and the vast, dark plains of Africa help clarify her state of mind at the beginning of the film? Or were we wasting valuable film time? Denmark finally won out, but what appears here and in the film is in fact a compressed version of what Kurt originally wrote. I do not think that what is here, what we filmed, is better than what was originally written, but it is shorter and seems to accomplish the contrast we felt was needed.

There is an old Hollywood axiom that says, "If you can't tell it in two sentences it's not worth telling." It's the subject of many jokes, but as in most clichés there is an awful lot of truth in the axiom. We spent two years trying to find the "spine" or "armature" of this piece, trying to distill the idea down to one or two clear sentences that would be a guidepost. We finally settled on *Possession. Freedom versus obligation. If I say I love you, what price am I expected to pay? To what extent am I obligated?* Trivial as it may sound, it's important to me to be able to describe the heart of a film simply and evocatively in order to test each scene, character, and development against that idea. It forces some linear sense of where the hell we're going and provides some real discipline. It makes the film cohesive to me, though I don't believe for a moment that a writer needs to write with this armature in mind. It's something to discover with the screenwriter during the work process. What finally became the armature was the first idea Kurt had mentioned in our initial work session, but we circled around and around trying to improve on it before coming all the way back to where we had begun. The idea of possession seemed to be organic to both the foreground story of Karen's relationships and the background story of colonialism. It seemed to knit together her relationships with the Africans as well as with her husband and her lover. It became an important track for us to follow and led us to try to dramatize her attempts at "possession" with her pond and dam, her china, her attempts to make Europe out of Africa. By contrast, it gave Finch Hatton a clear conflict with her. It also provided anchor points for an arc, as near the end of the film she begins to let go of these possessions one by one.

As in every case in which a film is based on literary material, selection is a major problem. What stays and what goes? In this case we had to deal not only with Karen's love affair with Africa, but with the stories of her arranged marriage to Bror and of her love affair with Finch Hatton. Each of these elements might have occupied an entire screenplay. Those who have read the book know there are many beautiful and lengthy chapters describing events of her life with her houseman Farah Aden and with Kamante, the young boy who became her renowned chef. It was necessary, in the film, to try to make two or three scenes create the impact of these prose passages.

Among the writers who previously had done drafts of this material for earlier attempted productions of *Out of Africa* is Judith Rascoe, a very gifted writer and a friend. I inherited two of her drafts with the project and we incorporated some of her material into this final version. The scene with Denys and Karen making love—*Don't move, I want to move*, and his repeated *Don't move*—is from Rascoe. Another of her ideas was to have Bror break the news of Denys's death to Karen. In fact, he didn't, but for film purposes it seemed to Kurt and me that Rascoe's invention was much more economical than the facts and dramatically much better.

Another of the old Hollywood axioms is "Good books make bad movies and bad books often make good ones." While this, of course, is not always true, it points to the fact that filmmakers often lose the very thing that attracts them to a good book—its writing style, the tone and prose of the author. Although we spent days trying, we were unable, with one exception, to lift passages from the book intact and use them in the film. This forced us to come up with a "voice" for Karen that was constructed especially for the film—one that would sound authentically like hers and blend seamlessly with the passage from the book we *did* use. This was especially difficult when it came to Karen's monologues.

The film is broken into six sections, or acts, which are enclosed and separated by seven monologues or "voice-overs"—Karen speaking directly to the audience, as if she were writing. Six of these had to be invented. For purposes of clarity, I've listed these sections and monologues, which provide a basic outline of the film.

A. The *Opening Monologue* ("He was waiting for me there.")
   1. *Act One*—ends with Bror's departure for war
B. The *War Monologue* ("And if we're tested at all, it's for patience.")
   2. *Act Two*—through her journey to the front, whipping the lions, and her visit with Bror in the tent, which changes their relationship
C. The *Compass Monologue* ("I had a compass from Denys, to steer by, he said.")
   3. *Act Three*—from her discovery of syphilis to her departure from Africa to be treated
D. The *Memory of Africa Monologue* ("I stayed in this room in Rungstedlund and tried to remember the colors of Africa.")
   This monologue and the visual montage under it divide the film into its two main sections
   4. *Act Four*—from her return to Africa, finding it a home for the first time, through her separation from Bror, her safari and courtship with Denys, and Denys's decision to move in with her
E. The *Denys Moves In Monologue* ("In the days and hours that Denys was at home, we spoke of nothing small or ordinary.")
   5. *Act Five*—glimpses of their life together, including intimations of his departure, through her financial hard times, her gradual estrangement from Denys, the fire, Denys's death, and, finally, the funeral
F. The *Song of Africa Monologue* ("If I know a song of Africa . . .")
   This is the one monologue we were able to lift intact from the

book.

6. *Act Six*—from her goodbye to the farm, the goodbye to Kamante, through the gentlemen at the men's bar toasting her, and her farewell to Farah Aden

G. The *Lions on the Grave Monologue* ("The mail has come today, and a friend writes this to me . . .")

There are *pieces* of this letter that were taken from the book.

I know I should discuss length, but as I write the word I get a headache. I've never had, and hope never again to have, such a problem with the length of a picture. No matter what we did with it, it got longer. There are instances described in the footnotes of scenes that were shot and then deleted at the last minute during editing because of the film's length. Some of these scenes were particularly difficult to cut because they worked so well on their own. What is often surprising, however, is how much seems to remain of what has been cut. It's almost as though scenes melt a bit onto each other and when one scene is eliminated, some of what has been cut stays behind and touches the scenes that bordered it.

For those interested in legal trivia, my contract called for a film of *not more than two hours, fifteen minutes*. To violate this (which I did) would theoretically mean I would lose control of the picture—or, more precisely, lose the much-protected final cut. Eight weeks before the premiere of the film I showed Frank Price, the president of Universal Pictures and the man really responsible for this film, a cut of almost three hours. Given the kind of man Frank is, however, there was no discussion whatsoever of my violation of the length clause of the contract. We spoke only of possible improvements. I am as pleased for Frank Price as I am for myself that the film has been a success. Well . . . *almost* as pleased.

The aspiring screenwriter who happens on this text in the hope of some guidance with screenwriting format should not be misled by the amount of shot numbering and detailed visual description of camera angles. This is really a *shooting script*, prepared by the director, with the writer, after a lengthy work process. A first-draft screenplay need not, in fact probably should not, contain anywhere near this much detail. Although there are several schools of thought on this, most directors prefer less on the grounds that visualization is the director's department. Personally, I find it interesting to read what the writer has visualized and so do not mind a first draft that might be quite detailed in terms of shots. One is always safe submitting minimal shot description, the criterion being simple clarity—*Exterior* and *Interior* always indicated, and whatever description of place and/or props as necessary to indicate character.

One more personal note. Trying to make a film out of something that has become a classic piece of literature is worrisome. Making films in general is worrisome, but this one was more so. I did not want to be the one who finally brought *Out of Africa* to the screen only to have it turn out to be a lot of pretentious posturing in literary clothing, something that would violate all the basic principles of good moviemaking, beginning with "What is the story?" That we seem to have gotten away with it is due to this screenplay and the extraordinary actors who performed it.

Finally, the woman about whom we made this film is both Isak Dinesen and Karen Blixen. What Kurt has done is blend the *facts* of Karen Blixen's life as they were discovered by Thurman, and the *spirit* of Isak Dinesen's recollections as they were idealized by her in *Out of Africa*. He has managed to repeat the process by which she herself distilled the events of her life into meaning. As Thurman writes: "*Out of Africa* does not describe Karen Blixen's life on her African farm as it was, in a documentary sense, lived. The serene perfection of the style, the spareness of detail, the attendance of the Gods all signal that we have escaped from the gravity of practical questions and have gotten up into a purer element, one that offers less resistance to the ideal. The point of view in *Out of Africa* is the 'overview' which Karen Blixen called 'the one thing of vital importance to achieve in life.' What we see is a landscape from the air; time and action have been tremendously compressed and telescoped."

What follows is, in my experience, unusual: a screenplay that can be enjoyed as a piece of writing in and of itself. I think there is much to be learned from it by any aspiring screenwriter. I also think there is much to be enjoyed on the simple level of accompanying these characters as they move about in this lost world. But on these matters, I am extremely prejudiced.

Sydney Pollack
Fall 1986
Los Angeles

OUT OF AFRICA

THE SHOOTING SCRIPT

A   BLACK SCREEN

Faintly, MUSIC of Mozart. Slowly the SCREEN BRIGHTENS INTO:
THE AFRICAN PLAIN—SUNRISE. Vast, endless, shimmering.
SOUNDS of breathing, irregular, under stress.

B   EXT. A KILLING GROUND

Blurred movement; an animal SCREAM. SOUNDS of breathing
and MUSIC PERSIST.

C   CLOSE—AN OLD WOMAN IN BED

Her head rolls sharply toward us in a nightmare—

D   CLOSE—A YOUNG WOMAN (THE SAME) IN BED

Her head rolls sharply away from us in a gasp of pleasure.

SOUNDS of the animals struggling and the MOZART PERSIST.

E   EXT. THE AFRICAN PLAIN—DAWN

The landscape blood-red, lunar. A silhouette of an animal,
motionless. PAN to another animal, still also. Then another
and then . . . the figure of a MAN. As still as the other figures.
PUSH CLOSER.

                    OLD WOMAN (V.O.)
          He was an animal who loved Mozart . . . in-
          stinctively, without the need to know that it *was*
          Mozart . . .[1]

F   SHOT—A BRACELET—SILVER AND ELEPHANT HAIR

A MAN'S HANDS fastening it about a WOMAN'S WRIST.

                    OLD WOMAN (V.O.)
          He began our friendship with a gift.

                  KAREN'S VOICE
          What's this for?

                  MAN'S VOICE (DENYS)
          The story.

1

OLD WOMAN (V.O.)
It was the day after we met.

G   EXT. OPEN COCKPIT—KAREN—DAY

The airplane is climbing. The YOUNG KAREN pulls a pin out of
her hair. It streams freely behind her. The FAINT SOUND OF
WIND and still the Mozart.

OLD WOMAN (V.O.)
And later, not long before Tsavo, he gave me
another, an incredible gift: a glimpse of the world
through God's eye! And I thought: Yes, I see
. . . this is the way it was intended.

H   INT. A ROOM IN DENMARK—DAY

OPEN CLOSE on a vintage gramophone playing the Mozart.
PAN PAST a narrow bed—unmade, the pillow crumpled; a
night of troubled sleep. HOLD on Karen, older now, at a desk,
turned away, barely defined in the dim light.

OLDER KAREN (V.O.)
I've written about all the others, not because I
loved them less, but because they were clearer . . .

I   SHOT—KAREN AND DENYS—NIGHT

Dancing. A memory. Slightly slowed down. They seem to be
outside, surrounded by darkness.

OLDER KAREN (V.O.)
. . . easier. He was waiting for me there.

J   INT. THE ROOM IN DENMARK—OLDER KAREN—DAY

At her desk.

OLDER KAREN (V.O.)
But I've gone ahead of my story. He'd have hated
that. Denys loved to hear a story told well.

CAMERA MOVES TOWARD THE WINDOW, discovers a painting on
an easel: a lush green place, the antithesis of what WE SEE

2

THROUGH WINDOW: a flat, cold, gray landscape. Thin distant trees.

> OLDER KAREN (V.O.)
> You see . . . I had a farm in Africa at the foot of the Ngong Hills . . .

SOUND OF CORK POPPING. LAUGHTER.

1/2 OMITTED

3 EXT. A CORN-STUBBLE FIELD—DENMARK—DAY

HANS BLIXEN, in elegant tweeds, late twenties, drains his crystal goblet, holds it out to a BEAUTIFUL WOMAN to be refilled.

> BEAUTIFUL WOMAN
> It's too *cold* for champagne.

> HANS
> Too cold for anything *but*.

The woman moves on, leaving Hans alone with an angry KAREN, who is dressed in velvet shooting clothes.

> KAREN
> You said you'd be at Klampenborg.

> HANS
> I thought I'd come, but then I didn't. Was it fun?

She stares, hurt, turns on her heel. CAMERA FOLLOWS TO REVEAL: A dozen YOUNG PEOPLE, aristocratic. Shotguns, horses, carriages. SERVANTS with silver service, sandwiches. GAMEKEEPERS with dogs. PEASANT CHILDREN stare. It is a cold, gray November day as Karen moves through the shooting party, fumbling in her pouch for shells, near tears. She storms past BROR BLIXEN —Hans's identical twin!—joking with TWO GIGGLING SERVANT GIRLS.

> BROR
> (to Karen)
> Tanne!

3

She ignores him. He shrugs at the servant girls but then moves
to catch up, falling in beside her. He loads his shotgun, notices
she's been crying. They move in silence for a moment. Then:

> BROR
> Oh, come on: It's not as though you loved
> him— You'd like to be a baroness, that's all.

> KAREN
> He *lied* to me.

> BROR
> Of course! Would you be in bed with him other-
> wise? Hans is only dull, not stupid.

She glares at him . . . but now she grins, when a grouse
explodes before them. Bror just watches as Karen's on it,
swings. As she's about to shoot:

> BROR (continuing)
> Pretend it's Hans.

About to fire, she laughs instead. In one easy motion, Bror
swings, SHOOTS, drops the bird.

4   EXT. A STONE WALL—KAREN AND BROR—DAY

Sipping tea from a thermos. At distance a gamekeeper with
the dogs.

> BROR
> Where would you go?

> KAREN
> Anywhere. America. Ceylon. I'd even go to Aus-
> tralia. I've *got* to be away from here.

> BROR
> I'll give you all *I've* got—that should get you into
> town.
> (then)
> God, it was fun. Money.

> KAREN
> (long pause)
> Bror— *You* could marry me.

4

BROR

I'm determined to marry a virgin. I can't stand criticism.

KAREN

For the money, I mean.

BROR

Oh. Probably.

She sits forward, conviction building.

KAREN

Bror, look at us. I've got no life. They wouldn't teach me anything useful—now I've failed to marry. You know the punishment for that: "Miss Dinesen's at home." And *you've* gone through all your money—now you're off seducing the servant girls. We're a set! At least we're friends. We might be all right. If we weren't . . .
(shrugs)
. . . at least we'd've *been* somewhere!

BROR
(dry)
You don't think you're being too romantic.

KAREN

I've tried that!

BROR
(quieter)
Tanne? . . . Am I supposed to think you're serious . . . ?

As she gazes at him, we hear the shrill screech of a TRAIN WHISTLE. Then:

OLDER KAREN (V.O.)
I had a farm in Africa . . .

5/18 OMITTED

5

19   EXT. THE AFRICAN PLAIN—VERY WIDE—DAY

MAIN TITLE BEGINS. Through FOREGROUND, a rickety train: an engine, two native cars, two flatcars with crates stenciled "BLIXEN," and last a first-class car.

> OLDER KAREN (V.O.)
> (quieter)
> I had a farm in Africa at the foot of the Ngong Hills . . .

20   LOW TRAVELING SHOT—THE TRAIN (AERIAL)

Small against the landscape. MOVE IN TO FIND Karen with her deerhound (Dusk) on the rear platform, captivated. TITLES CONTINUE.

> OLDER KAREN (V.O.)
> (quieter still)
> . . . I had a farm in Africa . . .

20a   THE TRAIN—LATER

New terrain. New animals. Perhaps a lion on a kill. TITLES.

20b   THE TRAIN—LATE AFTERNOON

As the day ebbs away. Rhino, zebra, impala, elephant, warthog. Karen still transfixed. TITLES CONTINUE.

21   OMITTED

22   EXT. MT. KILIMANJARO—THE TRAIN—SUNSET

As the sun moves behind the majestic mountain, the tiny train passes low in the frame. TITLES CONTINUE.

22a   EXT. THE PLAIN—TRAIN—NIGHT

Last light. Forcing Karen inside the kerosene-lit car. The train recedes into the darkness, its taillights winking red and green. END MAIN TITLES.

22b. ANGLE—THE TRAIN—DAY

Rushing TOWARD CAMERA, BRAKES SCREECHING, throwing SPARKS.

22c EXT. REAR PLATFORM—KAREN—DAY

Barefoot, disheveled, she gapes at Denys and KANUTHIA, his half-wild gun bearer and tracker, each with a rifle and bedroll and each holding an enormous tusk. As he passes:

> DENYS
> Good morning.

> KAREN
> Have you had trouble?

> DENYS
> Now and then . . . Have you?

> KAREN
> I'm . . . traveling to Nairobi.

> DENYS
> You've caught the right train. Excuse me.

He moves past her toward the flatcar. She goes into her car, moves through to the other platform, watching as Denys and Kanuthia load the ivory. Natives from their cars JABBER and clamber over Karen's crates, trying to inspect the huge tusks.

> KAREN
> Get away from there! Shoo!

The natives look up. Denys stops dead.

> DENYS
> Shoo?

> KAREN
> That's all my crystal. My Limoges.

> DENYS
> Ahh. They didn't know it was Limoges.

7

                        (in Swahili)
Come down now.
                        (to Karen)
You plan to stay, then.

                        KAREN
I've come out to marry Baron Blixen, do you
know him?

                        DENYS
Bror. Another farm, isn't it?

                        KAREN
We plan to start a dairy— Are you quite famous?
They stopped the train for you.

                        DENYS
It's rude not to, here. Are you sure we need a
dairy?

                        KAREN
I should've thought.

                        DENYS
It seems soon for that—milk at the door.

The train TOOTS, begins to move.

                        KAREN
Aren't you boarding?

                        DENYS
No, I'm going on.

Karen looks in bewilderment at the emptiness around her.
The following is SHOUTED:

                        KAREN
On to *where*?

                        DENYS
If you'll mention the ivory to Berkeley Cole!
—Bror knows him!

KAREN
(waving)
I'm . . . Baroness Bixen!

DENYS
Not yet!—Finch Hatton! Denys George!

He and Kanuthia turn in unison, fall easily into a loping
stride across the African plain.

22d INT. NAIROBI TRAIN SHED—DAY

A cloud of STEAM FADES to reveal the black face of FARAH
ADEN, a turbaned Somali, haughty, inscrutable. PULL BACK TO
SEE Karen moving through the debarking natives with Dusk.
She searches for Bror.

FARAH
Msabu. I am Farah Aden. We can go now.

KAREN
Where is Baron Blixen?

FARAH
He is at Muthaiga, msabu.

Farah turns, walks away. Puzzled, she follows.

22e EXT. NAIROBI STREET—DAY

Farah exits, followed by Karen. He hails a rickshaw. Dusk
growls at Farah, who looks back, impassive.

KAREN
(to Dusk)
Honestly!
(to Farah)
Where is Muthaiga?

FARAH
Muthaiga is a house, msabu. Where British go
for drinking.

Peremptory, he hands her into the rickshaw, stares at the dog,
SPEAKS to the boy in Swahili.

9

KAREN

Listen: on the train? I have *crates*. There is *crystal*. And *china*—do you know *chi-na*?

FARAH

Yes, msabu. China. It can break.

Dusk jumps into the rickshaw as Karen is borne away.

22f FULL VIEW—NAIROBI STREET—DAY

Tin roofs, sidewalk stalls, a mixture of races and tribes. Some Asian. Karen's rickshaw moves through.

22g TRAVELING WITH KAREN AND DUSK

She swelters in the heat, dress clinging, hair damp. Dusk's in a frenzy.

22h KAREN'S P.O.V.—TRAVELING

A bare-breasted woman, so black she shines. A woman with her teeth filed to points. An occasional carriage with a white man.

22i LONG VIEW—THE RICKSHAW

Disappearing, bearing Karen off.

22j EXT. MUTHAIGA CLUB—ESTABLISHING—DAY

Cool and green. Carriages, native boys tending horses. Dusk lies panting at the door. Far-off PEALS OF LAUGHTER, the SOUNDS OF LAWN TENNIS.

22k INT. MUTHAIGA CLUB—LOBBY—KAREN—DAY

Deserted, still. A reception desk. Mail slots. Room keys. Battered furniture, well-thumbed newspapers. On the walls, small celebrations of the empire. CONVIVIAL NOISE from the bar o.s. Karen moves toward it.

22l INT. MEN'S BAR—DAY

Military plaques, artillery shells. Men drink at tables and bar,

10

throw darts. A HUGE MAN reads a newspaper. Karen enters, hesitates.

> KAREN
> Excuse me? . . . Can someone tell me where I'd
> find Baron Blixen?

The room falls silent; the men stare.

> HUGE MAN
> Kaninu!

And returns to his paper. KANINU, a black majordomo, moves from the bar to deal with her.

> KANINU
> Memsaabs must not be here.

> KAREN
> I'm simply trying to find someone.

> KANINU
> Memsaabs must not be here.

Without touching her, he firmly escorts her out.

22m INT. LOBBY—KAREN—DAY

> Angry, humiliated, she's at a loss when:

> BROR (O.S.)
> Tanne! Where have you been?

PULL BACK to reveal Bror bounding down the stairs.

> KAREN
> Where have *you* been?

A hasty embrace.

> BROR
> Arranging things. How was the trip—you can
> tell me later— Would you like to change?

11

KAREN

My luggage is still on the train.

Farah enters with her cases.

BROR
(to Farah)
Room D, Farah, head of the stairs.
(to Karen)
I haven't done anything about a ring, d'you care?

KAREN

Did you think I wouldn't come?

BROR

Didn't know if you'd want to spend the money.
You'll love it here—servants are wonderful, and
we pay them almost nothing. Shall we get a
drink? We've got an hour before the wedding.

KAREN

An hour!

22n EXT. THE WIDE LAWN—DAY

Buffet tables, punch bowls, servants with silver trays. Fifty
GUESTS, colonists, pioneers, individuals all. The crowd begins
to converge at the patio doors as BAGPIPES SCREECH a truly
awful "Wedding March." CAMERA TRACKS to Karen and Bror
in the doorway, about to step outside. She's lovely, rushed,
apprehensive.

BROR

You ought to have a hat, Tanne.[2]

KAREN

I don't look— Good Lord, the ivory; I've got this
man's ivory!

BROR

—Whose ivory?

22o THE LAWN—WIDE

12

A boisterous crowd. CRIES of "Run for it, Blix!" and "Don't promise a thing!" Scattered APPLAUSE for Karen. Two men on horseback, fresh from polo, drift through. A woman with a baby, a lethal revolver holstered on her hip. A vivacious woman, her neck and jaw scarred by claws. Fly whisks on some wrists, a drink in every hand. Bror grins and greets, grabs a glass of champagne, downs it, knows everyone. Karen is wan, a stranger. They move to SIR HENRY BELFIELD, governor of the colony. His wife, LADY SARAH, steps to Karen's side, volunteering as her matron.

> LADY SARAH
> I'm Sarah, Lady Belfield. Shall I stand up for you?

> KAREN
> Thank you.

The "WEDDING MARCH" ENDS.

> SIR HENRY
> Short or long, Blix?

> BROR
> Long, please. Give me time to adjust to it.

> SIR HENRY
> Settle down, all!
> (rapidly)
> By the authority of Her Majesty's Government vested in me—
> (a chorus of boos)
> I declare that the Baron Bror von Blixen, citizen of Sweden, and—
> (low, to her)
> What's your name, my dear?

> LADY SARAH
> Dammit, Henry, I told you her name.

> KAREN
> Karen Christentze Dinesen.

13

SIR HENRY

Karen Christianson Dinesen, a female subject of
the king of Denmark, are henceforth united man
and wife. God save this company—God save the
king.

A number of echoing "God save the kings." PUSH IN ON Bror
and Karen. He kisses her.

KAREN
(quietly)
Thank you for this.

BROR
(a grin)
Baroness.

22p THE PARTY—TRACKING SHOT—DAY

THREE WOMEN, looking off to Bror and Karen.

ONE WOMAN
He's *such* fun: what a shame if she coops him up.

MOVE to a group of MEN. As we pass:

FIRST MAN
—silly fool thinks he can force the railroad all
the way to Uganda. Nothing there, anyway.

SECOND MAN
Nothing here, either, was there?

MOVE TO LORD DELAMERE, hair to his shoulders, in a male
group, all in hats.

DELAMERE
There's nothing they need; why should they
work? Teach the native things to want, *then* he'll
work![3]

He's caught sight of Karen and Lady Belfield.

DELAMERE (continuing)
Hello, Sarah. Where's your muddleheaded husband?

14

LADY SARAH

The *governor*'s at the punch bowl, thank you very much, hoping to avoid you. Would you like to meet the bride, or did you come just for the whiskey?

DELAMERE

Not the company, God knows.

LADY SARAH

Baroness Blixen, may I present Lord Delamere. Such as he is.

KAREN

Lord Delamere.

DELAMERE

Baroness. Swedish, are you?

KAREN

Danish, actually.

DELAMERE

Ahh, the *little* country—next to Germany . . . If it comes to war, where will Denmark stand?

KAREN

On its own, I hope. We have that history.

DELAMERE

Mmm. Is there something we can call you that gets us 'round this "Baroness"?

KAREN

What do they call you, Lord Delamere?

DELAMERE

D., if I'm lucky.

22q FULL SHOT—PARTY—DAY—LATER

Drunker. Afternoon shadows. Two boys fight hard, ignored. The huge man from the bar is there. MOVE PAST a MIXED GROUP as a man drops ice in a woman's bodice. Another MAN

15

reaches after it. The woman does not object.

CAMERA CONTINUES, HOLDS on Karen, alone at the battered buffet table, wilting. FELICITY, fifteen, athletic, a tomboy, revolver in her waistband, sips champagne, comes to Karen.

> FELICITY
> My stupid name's Felicity, but I do like your dress.

> KAREN
> Thank you.

> FELICITY
> You ought to have a hat, though.[4]

> KAREN
> So I'm told. I don't look well in hats.

> FELICITY
> We die of sunstroke here.

> KAREN
> Be sure they don't bury me in a hat, will you?

> FELICITY
> (grins)
> Right-o.
> (beat)
> Are you nervous?

> KAREN
> Should I be?

> FELICITY
> (colors)
> You know . . . wedding night and all.

22r WIDE OVER THE LAWN—DUSK

Someone FIRES a Very pistol: the flare casts an eerie light. It REVEALS an amorous couple, a DRUNK passed out on the grass, and Karen alone, searching for Bror. She looks off:

22s ACROSS THE LAWN—BROR AND A WOMAN (VICTORIA)

16

He stands laughing with the full-bodied Victoria. Their manner is familiar as Karen steps INTO THE SHOT.

> VICTORIA
> So they're both of them naked and not a shrub
> in sight—

> BROR
> —Karen. Have you met Vicky Gresham?

> VICTORIA
> Hello, Baroness. I'd curtsy but I'm drunk.

> KAREN
> (to Bror)
> May I see you, please?

> VICTORIA
> Excuse me—

She moves off hastily. Bror turns to Karen.

> BROR
> If you want any friends, Tanne, I'd make them
> here. There *is* no one else.

> KAREN
> I want to see my house.

> BROR
> There are people traveled half a day for this
> party; in a month you'll kill to be asked to another.

> KAREN
> I want to see my house.

> BROR
> (beat; quiet)
> You may want to change; it's a two-hour ride.

22t INT. MUTHAIGA CLUB CORRIDOR—KAREN—NIGHT

As she moves toward her room, she sees one of the tusks on

17

the floor outside another room, the door slightly ajar. She moves to the room, knocks softly.

22u INT. DENYS'S ROOM—NIGHT

We hear Karen's VOICE: "Excuse me?" The door opens; she enters. A bamboo filament light on a desk. A gun rack, some sheet music by Schubert, many books, a print of the Montgolfier balloon.

> MAN'S VOICE
> My God, these people drink!

KAREN whirls to see BERKELEY COLE, delicate, gently drunk, leaning against the door, holding the other tusk.

> KAREN
> I'm sorry, I was just—you've caught me snooping.

> BERKELEY
> He won't mind. That's a thing about Denys: he doesn't mind.

> KAREN
> Are you Berkeley Cole?

> BERKELEY
> Umm.

> KAREN
> I brought the ivory with me—on the train.

> BERKELEY
> Thank you, then. Are you taking your quinine?

> KAREN
> Yes . . .

She ought to leave, but her eyes linger on a small framed photo of a woman.

> BERKELEY
> An actress. Mad for each other, but her husband found them out—Denys had to kill him. It's the

18

gallows if he ever goes back.

                    KAREN
No . . .

                    BERKELEY
His sister actually.

                    KAREN
                (laughs, then)
He's got lovely books. Does he lend them?

Berkeley puts down the tusk, ambles over to the couch.

                    BERKELEY
We had this friend, Hopworth. He'd got a book
from Denys and didn't get it back. I said: Denys,
you wouldn't lose a friend for the sake of a silly
book? He said: No, but he has, hasn't he?
                (then)
Did you come out through London?

                    KAREN
No, I came through Rome.

                    BERKELEY
I thought you might have a newspaper.

                    KAREN
No . . . I'm sorry.

                    BERKELEY
Nothing in them, anyway.
                (beat)
I . . . had a friend . . . for the dances at Oxford.
They're in June, along the river. She always had
a new silk dress . . . I think you're wearing her
perfume.

Moment. Sympathetic, she holds her wrist close to his cheek.
SOUNDS of party; someone LAUGHS.

                    BERKELEY
                (continuing quietly)
No. It's very nice . . . but not the same.

                      19

FARAH (O.S.)
Msabu.

ANGLE ADJUSTS to include Farah at the door, judgmental.

FARAH (continuing)
We can go now.

23/36   OMITTED

37   EXT. A ROAD—NIGHT

Two ox wagons loaded with her crates, native drivers silent.
Farah on one wagon, Karen, dozing, with the dog on the
other. Bror on horseback.

38   CLOSE ANGLE—A NATIVE BOY—NIGHT

With a spear. He stares, steals away to take the news.

39   APPROACHING THE HOUSE—NIGHT

A few natives wait with torches. Now, from out of the dark,
more and more, the children running, CALLING, falling silent
when they're near. A KIKUYU MURMUR.

40   TRAVELING—KAREN AND WAGON—NIGHT

She holds the dog tightly, apprehensive.

41   KAREN'S P.O.V.—TRAVELING—NIGHT

Kikuyu staring, some walking silently with the wagon.

42   AT THE HOUSE—FULL SHOT—NIGHT

A dour white man, BELKNAP, pushes through the crowd. Bror
helps Karen down. She is uncomfortable with the silence.
Bror speaks sharply in Swahili: from the throng, a jagged
"Jambo, Memsaab!"

BROR
This is Belknap, Karen; he runs the farm.

20

BELKNAP
Evening, ma'am.

BROR
And here's your cook: name's Esa.

Old and grizzled, ESA bows.

BROR (continuing)
And this one's Juma. Houseboy, but he'll do all
work.

JUMA's young, anxious, manages a shy:

JUMA
Jambo, Memsaab.

KAREN
. . . Juma.

BROR
Come see your house.

43   INT. LIVING ROOM—NIGHT[5]

Bror and Farah hold kerosene lamps as Karen steps in. It is
clean, quite bare, only Bror's necessities. An antipathy between
Farah and the dog.

BROR
Dining room's there, and the bedroom's to the
back. Kitchen's outside, to keep the house cool.
There's even a bath.
(beat)
It's really quite nice, Tanne. For Africa.

44   INT. DINING ROOM—CLOSE—CANDLES—NIGHT

Illuminating a bare table. Karen's bathed, wears a dressing
gown. She and Bror finish a late supper. Juma stands immo-
bile at the wall, staring at the dog.

KAREN
When you leave me, I'm going to marry Berkeley Cole.

21

                         BROR
                        (grins)
A man in trade?

                         KAREN
Is that what he does?

                         BROR
He's thick with the Somalis. Crowd of 'em up on
his land who think he's some sort of prince. He
sells Finch Hatton's ivory.

                         KAREN
Belknap's a cheery sort.

                         BROR
Had a place of his own. Went belly-up trying to
grow flax.

                         KAREN
Does he know cattle?

                         BROR
. . . I didn't buy cattle. We're going to grow
coffee instead.

Moment. She's stunned. She waits, then, cool:

                         KAREN
That's not what we planned.

                         BROR
You were in Denmark. I had to decide.

                         KAREN
We'd *made* a decision. We don't know anything
about coffee.

                         BROR
You plant it, it grows.

                         KAREN
We *said* we'd do a dairy. My mother put her
money for—

22

BROR

Your mother doesn't care whether it's cows or
coffee as long as it pays. You've got to be with a
herd or things go wrong. I didn't come to Africa
to sit with silly cows.
(shrugs)
Just tell her we changed our minds.

KAREN

Next time you change your mind, do it with *your*
money!

BROR

They bought you a title, Baronessa—they didn't
buy me.

Moment. Idly, Karen touches the candle flame with her finger,
licks it. Then:

KAREN

Juma? Fetch some wine . . .
(then)
. . . for my lover's brother.

Juma goes. Bror wipes his mouth, gets up.

BROR
(as he passes)
I think you're tired, Karen.

KAREN

Did I tell you Hans came to say goodbye?

He grabs her hair close to her head, yanks her up.

BROR
(close)

Be careful . . .

He shoves her into the table. She comes at him with the candle,
wax dripping. He knocks it away, SWEARING, batting at his
pants.

Slow, he comes for her—she might spring at him! He grabs

23

her arms. A low cry—and then he kisses her brutally. The dog GROWLS, about to spring. They break. She hits him with her fist. A long moment of silence . . . then slowly, defiant, she undoes her belt, drops it. Her gown falls open. Contemptuously, she pushes past him. He follows. Juma returns, rights a glass. The SOUND OF A LOUD DOOR SLAM. Juma doesn't spill a drop.[6]

45   EXT. HOUSE—CLOSE—FARAH—DAY

Barking orders in Swahili, as several Kikuyu unload the wagons. DOLLY with a crate as they take it toward the house. Karen comes out in a robe, sipping tea.

> KAREN
> Where is Baron Blixen?

> FARAH
> He is gone to hunt, msabu.

> KAREN
> Did he say when he'd be back?

> FARAH
> He says he can come before the rain.

> KAREN
> (looks up)
> Is it going to rain today?

> FARAH
> . . . It can be many days before the rain, msabu.

A flicker of fear, then disbelief, then anger. She turns, goes quickly inside.

45a   INT. BEDROOM—KAREN—DAY

She storms in, throws open the closet doors, searches furiously, pulls out a suitcase, flings it on the bed. She throws a few things into the bag, jams it closed, picks it up, but has nowhere to go. A moment, then she sinks to the bed, out of breath, angrily wiping at her eyes.

24

She makes a decision, goes back to the closet, pulls out her finest riding clothes.

An ANIMAL SCREAM:

46   CLOSE ON A SCREAMING BABOON—DAY

Being pelted by clods of dirt. It scampers into the bush, pursued by NATIVE BOYS.

Karen and Belknap watch. She's on horseback, elegantly dressed, hatless—her manner brusque, determined.

> BELKNAP
> Ohio I'd put up scarecrows to keep the birds away—here you hope there's enough leopard to keep down the baboons. Course, they'll take your dog, too—

> KAREN
> (hard)
> —How much will we plant?

> BELKNAP
> A thousand acres, the Baron figured—

> KAREN
> (interrupting)
> —How long will that take?

> BELKNAP
> Depends on Kinanjui.
> (at her look)
> Chief of the Kikuyu. Have to deal with him to get your help.

> KAREN
> And when's our first harvest?

> BELKNAP
> These are seedlings . . . three—maybe four years.

> KAREN
> (stunned)
> —Four years?

BELKNAP

—If they bear at all. No one's ever tried coffee
this high.

KAREN

—What do we *live* on for four years?

BELKNAP

Miz Blixen?—I'm workin' to get home. If you
haven't got it, be good if you'd tell me now.

She looks about her. The sun beats down. She looks up at the
cloudless sky. Then:

KAREN

We'll plant five hundred.

47   OMITTED

48   INT. LIVING ROOM—KAREN AND FARAH—NIGHT[7]

Farah finishes unpacking a clock. Karen, sweat-stained, dirt
on her face, carries it to the mantel, winds it. The room is half
furnished, looking very European. She moves the hands of the
clock to the hour—it CUCKOOS. Farah stares.

49   EXT. STREAM—CLOSE—DUSK DRINKING—DAY

ADJUST ANGLE to see Farah listening as Karen GESTICULATES.

KAREN

. . . If you put a *dam* here to stop the water, I can
have a *pond*. Do you know how to make a *pond*?

FARAH

Msabu, this water must go home to Mombasa.

KAREN

It can go home later. After we've made a pond.

FARAH

Msabu, this water lives at Mombasa.

26

The TINKLE OF A BELL. She turns. CAMERA ADJUSTS to see a native boy, KAMANTE, leaning on a crude crutch, tending a herd of goats. He stares openly at her, his manner unafraid. His leg is ulcerated, ugly. She holds his gaze a moment, calls Dusk and moves off.

50   OMITTED

50a EXT. KIKUYU SHAMBAS—KINANJUI'S HUT—DAY

As KINANJUI, chief of the Kikuyu, bells in his elongated ear-lobes, his imperial head held high, steps out. PULL BACK to see Karen and Farah standing before him.

> KAREN
> (a speech)
> Chief Kinanjui, I have heard you are a wise chief and—

> FARAH
> —Msabu—

> KAREN
> (to Farah)
> Not now, Farah, please—
> (to Kinanjui)
> —and I look forward to our dealings. Your people are good workers, and I will deal with them honestly and fairly. I hope that we will prosper together, and in time I hope we may become friends.

Dead SILENCE. Uncomfortable. Karen looks to Farah:

> FARAH
> Msabu, this chief has no British.

> KAREN
> (beat)
> Tell him I am Baroness Blixen and—

> FARAH
> —This chief knows that, msabu.

27

                    KAREN
        Tell him . . . tell him what I said.

Farah speaks to Kinanjui in rapid Swahili. Kinanjui responds:
an excited, drawn-out speech; then he turns on his heel and
enters his hut.

                    KAREN
        What did he say?

                    FARAH
                  (hesitant)
        He says these Kikuyu can work, but this chief
        must have tobacco.

She stares at him, but he turns to move away. She follows,
puzzled. TRACK them through the shambas; goats being milked,
CHILDREN play, chickens run; maize is ground, old WOMEN
rake soil. Activity stops as they stare at the "Memsaab." Ahead
stands Kamante, leaning on his crutch. Karen passes him,
uncomfortable. Changes her mind, goes back, kneels.

                    KAREN
        Your leg is very sick. You must come to the house
        for medicine.

No response. A crowd gathers, deeply interested.

                    KAREN (continuing)
        If you do not come, the other boys will say you
        are afraid.
                  (beat, to Farah)
        Does he understand me?

                    FARAH
        Yes, msabu.

                    KAREN
                  (to Kamante)
        I myself will think only that you are foolish.

Kamante darkens. Some in the gathering GIGGLE.

                       28

KAREN
(continuing, to all, imperious)
This boy must come to my house for treatment.
See to it . . .

She moves off, her dignity regained. Farah follows, CAMERA
TRACKING. A long beat, then:

KAREN (continuing)
What else did Kinanjui say?

FARAH
. . . He says coffee must not grow this high.

Karen reacts but walks on, determined. Then:

FARAH (continuing)
Never mind, msabu, he is Kikuyu.

She almost smiles.

50b EXT. NAIROBI STREET—KAREN AND FARAH—DAY[8]
Farah drives, Karen rides as their wagon passes an unoccu-
pied new automobile, in the midst of the carriages and horses.

FARAH
This is a motorcar, msabu.

KAREN
I know that. What's it doing here?

FARAH
God is great, msabu.

50c INT. MUTHAIGA CLUB—LOBBY—KAREN—DAY[9]

Being handed her mail by an INDIAN FACTOTUM behind the
desk. She sorts through it: three letters, all for Bror.

She picks them up, wanders to the dining-room entrance. PAN
with her to SEE THROUGH THE DOORWAY; most tables occupied,
a number of people from the party, including Victoria, Delamere and Lady Delamere. No one is alone. As the MAÎTRE D'
approaches, Karen hesitates, then turns away.

29

50d EXT. COFFEE FIELDS—HIGH ANGLE ON KAREN—DAY[10]

She walks through rows of NATIVE WORKERS on their knees planting, supervised by Belknap. CRANE DOWN to her as she kneels, packs dirt tightly around one of the seedlings. The workers stare at her.

50e EXT. SOMEWHERE NEAR SHAMBAS—LONG SHOT—DAWN

Silhouetted against the orange sky, a row of Kikuyu women, bent double under their burdens of wood, like giant snails in the landscape.

50f INT. HOUSE—KAREN—DAWN[11]

Sipping tea, pacing, she passes the window, stops, looks off:

50g KAREN'S P.O.V.—THROUGH WINDOW[12]

The sky just pink. Kamante, stork-legged, leans on his crutch, alone, waiting.

                    KAREN'S VOICE
          Farah . . .

50h EXT. HOUSE—KAREN—DAY[13]

She moves to Kamante, followed by Farah, who carries alcohol and cotton. She kneels, wets the cotton.

                    KAREN
          This will hurt.

She touches the wounds with the cotton. He is stoic, just a flicker of pain. She notices.

                    KAREN (continuing)
          Tell me your name.

                    KAMANTE
          I am Kamante.

30

51   INT. KAREN'S BEDROOM—NIGHT

She lies in bed, her book put aside, staring off. She looks over at Bror's pillow, gets slowly out of bed.

51a   EXT. VERANDA—NIGHT[14]

Karen comes out, stands looking over the lawn. SOUNDS of the African night. From somewhere far off, the deep GROWL of a lion. Behind her Farah approaches out of the darkness with a shawl. He drapes it over her shoulder. A beat.

> FARAH
> It can rain someday now, msabu.

> KAREN
> (softly)
> Thank you, Farah.

52   INT. LIVING ROOM—EARLY MORNING

Fully furnished, immaculate: we might be in Paris. KAREN comes through in elegant riding clothes.

53   EXT. THE HOUSE—KAREN

Early and still. She rides away.

54   EXT. THE PLAIN—KAREN—DAY

Her rifle in its scabbard. She rides slowly, alert.

55   EXT. THORN TREES—DAY

Giraffes, quite close, bend to the tops of the trees and tower over her as she guides her horse gingerly through them. She is awed but apprehensive.

56   EXT. PLAIN—A CARCASS—DAY

A hyena struggles to keep a flock of vultures away from a half-eaten carcass. A short distance away, Karen observes. Her horse fidgets, so she veers away.

57   EXT. A HILLSIDE—KAREN—DAY

She sits elbows to knees, scans the plain with binoculars, her rifle in its scabbard. Her horse, ground-tied some distance away, WHICKERS. She ignores it.

58   ANOTHER ANGLE—A LIONESS—DAY

Bloody to the ears, stalks through the grass.

59   FULL SHOT—THE HILLSIDE

The horse SNORTS, WHINNIES, bolts. Karen scrambles up, wondering what frightened it, looks back and freezes. The lioness, stock-still, stares at her. Karen takes a step backward, ready to run.

> DENYS'S VOICE
> (flat, hard)
> Stand very still, please.
> (then)
> If you run, she'll think you're something good to eat.

CAMERA REVEALS Denys, rifle ready, some distance behind Karen. She dares not turn to see him.

> KAREN
> Do . . . you . . . have . . . a . . . gun?

> DENYS
> Yes . . . she won't like the smell of you.

> KAREN
> Finch Hatton?

> DENYS
> She's had her breakfast; see her big belly?

The lioness steps forward.

> KAREN
> For God's sake, shoot her!

32

DENYS
Let's give her a moment . . .

The lioness hesitates, then turns, tail swishing, and ambles off. Karen scrambles up, shaken, angry.

KAREN
Just how much closer did you plan to let her come?

DENYS
A bit. She wanted to see if you'd run. That's how they decide. A lot like people that way.

KAREN
She almost had me for lunch!

DENYS
Wasn't her fault, Baroness, she's a lion.

KAREN
Well, it wasn't mine!

DENYS
Doesn't that outfit come with a rifle?

KAREN
It . . . on my saddle.

DENYS
Better to keep it with you. Your horse isn't much of a shot.

He FIRES TWICE into the air, reloads once.

DENYS (continuing)
For Berkeley. We stopped at your house and then came looking. Are you all right?

Because she's gone white.

KAREN
Of course. I just—

But her knees buckle, and she's on the ground. He quickly kneels, pushes her head down.

> DENYS
> Stay down. Push up against my hand. Harder.

She doesn't faint. Kanuthia, spear loose in his hand, appears, leading Karen's horse.

> KAREN
> (gamely)
> I can ride.

60 EXT. KAREN'S TERRACE—DAY

Juma takes two bottles of wine from a straw-packed crate, Berkeley's gift—takes them into the house.

> KAREN
> (still distracted)
> Good Lord, you're sweet.

> BERKELEY
> You were on the road, actually. We're off to Magadi to shoot some ivory.

In b.g. a loaded safari wagon, mule drawn, two natives in attendance. Denys is wandering the garden, chatting in Swahili with Farah. Kanuthia stands off alone.

> BERKELEY
> (continuing, re: Denys)
> Has he made you sing yet?

> KAREN
> What . . . ?

> BERKELEY
> It's only a matter of time.

Denys arrives; Farah continues on into the house.

> KAREN
> Will you tell Berkeley what a fool I was?

34

DENYS
She had a lioness a bit interested.

KAREN
A bit?

DENYS
(shrugs)
It's all right to take a chance as long as you're the
only one who'll pay. Africa's very fair that way.

BERKELEY
(mixing drinks)
Where's Blix, anyway?

KAREN
Hunting.

BERKELEY
He been out long?

KAREN
. . . Yes.

BERKELEY
You'll need a good chat, then. Shall we stay to
supper, Denys?

Denys doesn't answer, may pretend not to have heard, looks
out over the landscape. Karen studies them.

KAREN
Do I have a say in this?

DENYS
(turning to her)
Yes . . .

KAREN
I'd like you to stay.

DENYS
Do you sing?

KAREN

Never.

DENYS

Can you tell a story, then?

KAREN

I happen to be very good at stories.

DENYS

I believe that.

60a HIGH ANGLE—THE NEW POND—DAY

Karen points, gestures. Berkeley and Denys watch, Dusk
scampers. At a discreet distance, Kanuthia.

DENYS (V.O.)

Where are your cows? For the dairy?

KAREN (V.O.)

We changed our minds. We'll grow coffee instead.

BERKELEY (V.O.)

Bit risky this high.

KAREN (V.O.)

So I've been told.

61 HIGH ANGLE—COFFEE FIELDS—THE THREE—DAY

Their figures tiny. Again at a distance, Kanuthia.

DENYS (V.O.)

Didn't fall for it, though, eh?

KAREN (V.O.)

I think they just haven't tried.

BERKELEY (V.O.)

Well, you've made your mark, Baroness.

KAREN (V.O.)

Every time I turn my back, it wants to go wild
again.

36

62   EXT. LAWN—CLOSE—DENYS—DUSK

A direct continuation in dialogue:

> DENYS
>
> It will go wild.

WIDEN to reveal the three of them strolling toward the house, past Kikuyu children squatting on the grass. Karen studies Denys a beat . . . she's distracted now by the figure of Kanuthia shadowing them.

> KAREN
>
> Your man . . . ?

> DENYS
>
> Kanuthia.

> KAREN
>
> He's not Kikuyu . . .

> DENYS
>
> No.

> KAREN
> (waits, then)
> Shall I see he's given supper?

> DENYS
>
> Don't do anything for him . . . Thank you, Baroness.

63   INT. DINING ROOM—DINNER—NIGHT

Candles, Karen in a gown. Juma pours wine, Denys and Berkeley in Bror's dinner jackets, particularly ill fitting on Berkeley.

> BERKELEY
>
> It's true of *all* Somalis—they're the *only* tribe that knows horses. *And* they don't drink, charge interest, chase other men's wives.

> DENYS
>
> He's got to come to the club for that.

Berkeley manages to dunk his sleeve in the gravy.

> BERKELEY
> Oops! God, Blix has long arms.

A plate slips from Juma's newly gloved hands. He looks apologetically at Karen, who tries to ignore it. Denys's reaction is harder to read.

> DENYS
> We ought to have a story now.

> KAREN
> All right. When I tell my nieces a story, one of them provides the first sentence.

> BERKELEY
> Anything?

> KAREN
> Absolutely anything.

> DENYS
> There was . . . a wandering Chinese named Cheng Huan, living in Limehouse . . . and a girl named Shirley . . .

> KAREN
> (challenged, she smiles)
> . . . who spoke perfect Chinese, which she had learned from her missionary parents.
> (then)
> Cheng Huan lived alone, in a room on Formosa Street, above the Blue Lantern. He sat at the window and in his poor, listening heart, strange echoes of his home and country would rebound.

During above her VOICE FADES, replaced by MUSIC. Perhaps HANDEL.

A SERIES OF IMAGES: Denys leans back, smiling, listening. CAMERA PANS OFF Berkeley to Karen telling the story.

38

INT. DRAWING ROOM—CLOSE—FIREPLACE—NIGHT

The flames flicker. PULL BACK to see a brandy glass, WIDEN FURTHER to find Denys curled on a cushion, listening. PAN TO Berkeley, entranced. CONTINUE TO Karen, standing quite still, telling the story. MUSIC FADES <u>DOWN</u> as Karen's VOICE FADES <u>UP</u>.

> KAREN
> . . . and next morning, they were found in the room above the Blue Lantern, the dead child and the warlord . . . with Cheng Huan's love gift coiled about his neck.

A beat. DENYS applauds slowly, BERKELEY joining.

> DENYS
> Had you been to those places?

> KAREN
> I've been a . . . mental traveler.

> BERKELEY
> Until now.

> DENYS
> (looking around)
> Isn't this England . . . Excuse me, Denmark?

She knows she's being chided.

> KAREN
> I like my things.

> DENYS
> When you traveled before, in your mind, did you carry so much luggage?

> KAREN
> A mental traveler doesn't have to eat or sleep. Or entertain.

> DENYS
> (smiles)
> You're right.

39

KAREN

Aren't you pleased that I brought my crystal and china?

DENYS

And your story, yes.

64   EXT. THE TERRACE—NIGHT

In the light of a single kerosene lamp on the millstone table, Denys and Berkeley, arm in arm, glasses in hands, sing Handel to a seated, radiant Karen.

65   EXT. MEADOW—CLOSE ON THEIR LEGS WALKING—NIGHT[15]

SOUND OF THEIR SINGING carries over, then FADES OUT. PULL BACK to see them strolling the meadow carrying drinks, enjoying the night. Denys reaches out his arm and stops them. They follow his gaze to:

66   THEIR P.O.V.—THE FOREST

Dappled in the moonlight, a herd of elephants. Great, gray, graceful shadows, walking along as though they had an appointment at the end of the world.

67   CLOSE ANGLE—DENYS, KAREN AND BERKELEY

Enchanted. Karen turns to whisper to Denys, doesn't, because he is lost to the elephants—and envy. As the herd moves off, a huge bull turns, scents the air a moment—RUMBLES.

DENYS
(quietly)
Yes, tembo. I see you.

68   EXT. THE HOUSE—FIRST LIGHT

OPEN ON Kanuthia, waiting with horses and wagon. ANGLE ADJUSTS: Berkeley, Karen and Denys approach from the house. Karen hugs Berkeley, Denys speaks to Kanuthia.

KAREN

I want you to come often.

40

BERKELEY

I'd like that very much.

He moves to his horse. Karen slowly approaches Denys.

KAREN

What is the etiquette? For saving my life; do I
say thank you?

DENYS

I didn't save your life. The lioness walked away.
There's a difference.

Barely a beat between them. He slips something off his wrist,
offers it to her: The bracelet we saw in F.

KAREN

What is this for?

DENYS

The story.

KAREN
(takes it)
It's lovely . . . Is it silver?

DENYS

Ethiopian.

KAREN
(hands it back)
My stories are free.

DENYS

Careful. I love to be told stories.

KAREN

Still, your present's much too dear.

DENYS

If you prefer things of no value . . . take my hat.

Perhaps he does some trick with the hat. She smiles.

                              KAREN
        Take care, Finch Hatton.

                              DENYS
        You wouldn't rather call me Denys?

A beat. Almost imperceptibly, she shakes her head no. He
studies her, nods; then:

                              DENYS (continuing)
        Baroness.

They move off slowly.

68a   CLOSE—KAREN—WATCHING

       PUSH TOWARD her as she watches them go. DROPS OF RAIN
       begin to fall, slowly at first . . . and slowly, she looks up.

69/77 OMITTED

78   EXTREME LONG SHOT—KIKUYU RUNNER—DAY

       Half naked, running TOWARD US, he seems to float as he leaps
       fallen logs. RAIN pelts the forest floor.

79   INT. DINING ROOM—KAREN—DAY

       O.S., the RAIN on the roof. It's dark. She trims the wicks of a
       half-dozen kerosene lamps. A BANGING O.S., an EXCHANGE OF
       SWAHILI. Farah enters.

                              FARAH
        He comes now, msabu. In the forest.

       She moves out quickly. HOLD on Farah, concerned.

80   EXT. A TWO-TRACK PATH IN THE FOREST—DAY

       Dark, very wet. Bror, mounted, tired, trailed by a mule wagon,
       scattered boys. He looks ahead.

                               42

81   BROR'S P.O.V.—KAREN

Standing ahead, soaked in her poncho, holding a rifle.

82   FULL SHOT—GROUP

As Bror reaches her. She stares up, wipes her face.

                    BROR
          What are you doing, Tanne?

                    KAREN
          . . . I want you to come home.

83   INT. BEDROOM—KAREN AND BROR—NIGHT

O.S. SOUND OF RAIN. Brass cartridges gleam beside perfume
bottles, lipstick, comb, and brushes on her vanity. In the mirror, the OUT-OF-FOCUS image of them in bed.

83a   INT. DRAWING ROOM—DAY (RAIN)[16]

CLOSE ON cuckoo clock. PAN TO the open doors, where three
NATIVE CHILDREN are watching the clock, waiting.

BROR enters, roaming the house, holding a beer and a sandwich. CAMERA MOVES with him to REVEAL Karen working at her
desk.

                    BROR
                  (moving)
          You've made yourself a home.

                    KAREN
          If you write, don't make too much of it—they're
          not thrilled about the cost of this coffee.

Bror moves out onto the veranda as Farah enters with ISMAIL,
a strong-eyed young man.

                    FARAH
          Msabu, this Somali is called Ismail. When you go
          where there are lions, he can bring your rifles.

43

KAREN

I don't need him to bring my rifles.

FARAH

It may be so, msabu. But he can bring your rifles.

KAREN

How much are we paying for this service which
I do not need?

FARAH

Five rupees, msabu.

KAREN

That's too much.

Bror wanders back in, listens.

FARAH

It may be so, msabu. But if sometime you are
torn in pieces and this Somali is not dead also,
he must always be gone from this place for the
fear that I can kill him. So I think it is not too
much.

He turns, escorts Ismail out. As they pass the clock it CUCKOOS,
the children giggle, flee.

BROR

What's all that about?

KAREN

Nothing . . . Berkeley Cole stopped by. With
Finch Hatton. They left some wine. I thought
we'd have some with dinner.

84   OMITTED

85   INT. DRAWING ROOM—NIGHT

CLOSE ON ANATOMY BOOK. PULL BACK to reveal Karen studying
it. In b.g., Bror is absorbed, repairing a rifle. They both sip
brandy. Karen stops reading, waits:

44

KAREN

Bror? We never spoke about children. Did you . . . ?

BROR

. . . Do you?

KAREN

Yes . . . Is that all right?

86   EXT. THE HOUSE—EARLY MORNING

As Karen comes out, ready to make the morning rounds. She
stops abruptly, stares off. CAMERA WHIPS TO SEE: a group of
Kikuyu natives, children, men and women, some with babies,
all waiting patiently on the lawn behind Kamante. Farah, arms
folded, turns to Karen:

FARAH

Msabu, these Kikuyu want to be sick now.

KAREN

. . . Good Lord . . .

87   EXT. LAWN—DAY—LATER

Karen kneels in front of Kamante, as the others wait.

KAREN

Your leg has got worse. You should go to hospital.

KAMANTE
(grave)

This leg may be foolish. It may think not to go to
hospital.

Bror has wandered out with his morning tea.

BROR

Don't start all this, Tanne, once they've got hold
of you they don't let go.

KAREN
(to Kamante)

This leg will do as it pleases. But if you will take

45

it to hospital I will think that you are wise . . .
and such a wise man as that I would want to
work in my house, for wages.

> KAMANTE
> (long beat)
I will speak to this leg.

88 EXT. OPEN PLAIN—A HORSEMAN—DAY

At full gallop, horse lathered, HOOVES POUNDING.

89 EXT. TWO-TRACK PATH—MOTORCYCLE WITH SIDECAR—DAY

It careens over the rough track. The passenger in the sidecar
cradles two rifles. They ROAR PAST CAMERA.

90 EXT. DIRT ROAD—A SPEEDING CAR—DAY

Topless, five armed men as passengers. It streaks PAST CAM-
ERA, spewing gravel.

91 EXT. NAIROBI STREET—DAY

Settlers on horses, in wagons, in carriages, hurry through
town. They clog the streets, the sidewalks. They wear hats,
bandannas, shorts, jackets, carry pistols, rifles, knives, shotguns.
Natives scurry out of the way. An old Ford tows an even older
howitzer.

92 INT. MUTHAIGA CLUB—MEN'S BAR—DAY

The room is packed. Delamere stands on a bench. Bror is
near the front, Berkeley and Denys at rear.

> FIRST MAN
The war's in Europe! How do we know it will
come this far?

> DELAMERE
German East is only two hundred miles south,
and Von Lettow is there. I don't want to wait till
they've joined us in the bar!

46

BROR
Would we engage them, then?

DELAMERE
(not unkindly)
Blix—it's our war. You're not really obligated
here, but thanks.

Bror colors.

SECOND MAN
I've got crops coming!

DELAMERE
We're all like that. We'll each have to stay and go
as we must.

FIRST MAN
They won't fight if we won't fight!

THIRD MAN
We could arm the Masai. Point them south.

Denys turns quietly—leaves. Berkeley is aware.

DELAMERE
Do *you* want the job collecting rifles from the
Masai when this is over?

BERKELEY
Will *they* use native troops?

DELAMERE
I'd assume . . .

Strong reaction in the room.

DELAMERE (continuing)
But not Masai.
(then)
Berkeley? What about your Somalis?

47

The club in b.g., they move against last-minute-arriving settlers.
Dialogue plays as continuation from above:

> BERKELEY
> They'd make fine scouts. We could cover the
> area from here to the border, gather informa-
> tion for when the Regular arr—

> DENYS
> What is it about? Have you any idea?

> BERKELEY
> . . . Not really.

> DENYS
> Then why do you want to get into it?

> BERKELEY
> Denys . . .

> DENYS
> —It's got nothing to do with us, Berkeley. They've
> made agreements we don't even know about—

> BERKELEY
> I imagine.

> DENYS
> —Victoria and the Kaiser were *cousins*, for God's
> sake; they divided Africa between them! You
> know why there's a border? Because she had
> *two* mountains and he had none—so she gave
> him Kilimanjaro! It was a silly argument between
> two spoiled-brat countries!

> BERKELEY
> Denys, the sooner we do this, the sooner it will
> end and we can pick up where we left off.

> DENYS
> (quietly)
> We're not going to pick up where we left off.

BERKELEY
Denys . . . we're *needed*.

PUSH IN to Denys's troubled face.

93a INT. DRAWING ROOM—BROR AND KAREN—DUSK

He's packing ammunition, guns. Farah moves in and out of
the room with tinned food, cooking utensils.

KAREN
You *don't* have to go—you want to go!

BROR
We've got to live here, Tanne.

KAREN
They've made it plain they don't want you!

BROR
They don't know where we stand. I'll have to
show them, that's all.

KAREN
I'm not so fond of their empire I'd have you
shot for it.

BROR
More likely chewed on than shot. The farm'll
take care of itself, and you've got Belknap.

KAREN
The farm does *not* take care of itself, and that's
not the point. I didn't expect to like you so much.

BROR
(grins)
You're not going to go falling in love?

Farah picks up his bags, starts out. Bror picks up the rest and
moves out, followed by Karen.

94 EXT. THE HOUSE—DUSK

As they come out. Farah puts the supplies on the pack mule.
There are two horses, and two natives waiting.

> BROR
> If you need me, send a runner to find Delamere
> —that's where I'll be.
> (kisses her)
> That's a fine kiss goodbye.

> KAREN
> I'm better at hello.

He mounts, moves off. As she watches:

> OLDER KAREN (V.O.)
> It's an odd feeling: farewell. There's some . . .
> envy in it. Men go off to be tested. For courage.
> And if we're tested at all, it's for patience, for
> doing without . . . perhaps for how well we can
> endure loneliness . . . But I'd always known that.
> It didn't require a war.
> (then)
> I said goodbye to Bror . . . Denys left without a
> word. Which was . . . quite proper.

95   EXT. FRENCH MISSION HOSPITAL—DAY

Inside the rough gardens, Karen turns Kamante over to a
nun. Karen touches him as she leaves. Hobbling on his crutch,
he turns a moment to stare back.

95a   EXT. COFFEE FIELDS—KAREN—SUNSET

She walks slowly, thoughtfully, along the neat rows of growing
seedlings, Dusk following behind her.

96   EXT. THE HOUSE—FELICITY—DAY

On horseback, a gutted gazelle across her pommel.

> FELICITY
> Hello the house!

50

Juma hastens out to take away the horse and carcass, Karen following. Dusk fussing over Felicity.

> KAREN
>
> Felicity!

> FELICITY
>
> Thought you might want some meat.

> KAREN
>
> Is there any word?

> FELICITY
>
> Nothing new. There's not much fighting. Awful fever, though.

She's uncomfortable. Karen waits. Then:

> FELICITY (continuing)
>
> I've got time for tea, I guess.

97   EXT. VERANDA—KAREN AND FELICITY [17]

Tea service on the millstone table; Karen, pouring, waits.

> FELICITY
> (after a beat)
>
> Are you for the Germans?

> KAREN
>
> Did they send you to ask me that?

> FELICITY
>
> We had a row about it in town.

> KAREN
>
> Whose side are you on?

> FELICITY
> (long beat)
>
> Yours . . .

> KAREN
>
> I'm not for the Germans.

51

FELICITY

They want to send me home to school. Mother
says I'm growing up wild. I wanted to ask you
about it.

KAREN

Me?

FELICITY

Well, you've been . . . around and about. Someday I'd like to run my own show, the way you do.

KAREN

Is that what I do?

FELICITY

You don't seem to need us much.
(beat)
Denys says he was in school for years and never
learnt a thing until Africa.

KAREN

I see.
(beat)
The world's smaller than Africa, but I think you
ought to see it. Make them teach you something
useful; they wouldn't do that for me. Then you
can stand alone. If you care to.

FELICITY

Do you like being alone?

KAREN

(beat, direct)

No.

FELICITY

Baroness . . . may I ask you something?
(silence)
It's about . . . about this . . . intercourse business.
(silence)
Is it . . . ? I'm sorry, I don't mean to be rude—
It's just— I've got nobody who'll be straight with
me.

KAREN

I didn't either . . . I suppose you ought to call
me Karen.

98 EXT. OX CORRAL—YOUNG OFFICER—DAY

As he speaks, PULL BACK to see Karen and Belknap treating a
sick bullock hobbled on the ground.

OFFICER

They need paraffin and tinned food. He wants
you to send a white man with a wagon.

Belknap is immediately wary.

KAREN

Is he all right?

OFFICER

I assume. Well enough to send the message.

KAREN

Where would my husband like this wagon sent?

OFFICER

He's with Delamere. On the border near Lake
Natron. That's confidential, of course.

KAREN

I'll bear that in mind.

OFFICER

Sorry, I only meant—It wouldn't do for it to be
talk around Nairobi—and we're going to *have* to
move you into town. We can't protect you here.

KAREN

What do you mean, move me into town?

OFFICER

With the men gone, we're worried about the
native element. We've orders: women and children into town.

53

KAREN

That's internment! And I'm a Danish subject,
Lieutenant.

OFFICER

Women and children, Baroness.

KAREN

Is that one category or two?

OFFICER

You'll want time to gather your things— I'll have
an escort here for you Thursday . . . and I'm a
captain, Baroness.

He mounts, rides out. Karen turns to Belknap:

BELKNAP

I'm not paid to fight, Miz Blixen.

KAREN

No . . .
                    (then)
Where is Lake Natron?

BELKNAP

South. Bush country. No place for a white man.

99   EXT. THE OPEN PLAIN—DAY

A freight wagon, four spans of oxen. Farah and Ismail walk,
Karen on horseback; Juma and two Kikuyu ride the wagon.
Two spare oxen herded by a third Kikuyu. Karen sweats in
the sun, swiping at flies.

She apprehensively checks a crude map, looks off ahead. We
see the contrast between the way Karen handles the heat and
the way the natives do: their calm tolerance, her anxiety.

100   EXT. CAMP—SUNDOWN

A single tent (hers). The oxen in a makeshift enclosure of
thorn bushes. Karen is sweat-stained, exhausted, studying her
map. A herd of wildebeest in the distance.

54

Farah and Ismail kneel on straw mats, salaam to the east, the red sky at their back.

101 EXT. <u>BLACK FRAME</u>—NIGHT

Nothing visible. SOUNDS of the African night. PAN and begin to see the camp; the fire, two natives eating, Juma bringing wood, Farah laying a head stool down, Ismail and others cleaning up.

In the distance, SEE Karen in her tent. PUSH CLOSER to her. She can barely keep her eyes open, and she eats out of a tin. She unbuttons the top of her shirt, her eyes drift closed, she crumples over.

102 EXT. DRY BANK—DAY

The oxen, eyes rolling, flanks heaving, stumbling in the spans, haul the wagon up the crumbling bank, the Kikuyu urging them on, using whips.

103 EXT. PLAIN—LONGEST VIEW POSSIBLE—DAY

Space. Distance. Sky. HOLD. From BEHIND CAMERA the caravan ENTERS THE FRAME, struggling forward.

104 INT. TENT—CAMP—KAREN—NIGHT

Naked but for trousers. She pours water from her canteen onto a cloth, sponges her face. Abrupt, the HOLLOW COUGH of a LION. She freezes, reaches for her shirt.

105 EXT. THE CAMP—NIGHT

She carries her bedroll from the tent to the fire where the natives lie, most of them asleep. She puts her bedroll among them, sees Farah awake, gazing at her.

> KAREN
> (whisper)
> We should have crossed a sand river today.
> (silence)
> I may have got us lost.

FARAH

God is great, msabu.

Suddenly she laughs. Covers her mouth, quickly.

106 EXT. THE CAMP—HIGH ANGLE—MORNING

Looking down from a hill. The camp asleep. Silence. Then the TINKLE of a small bell. A bare black leg moves THROUGH SHOT on horseback, BELLS on the ankle. Then nothing. Then the SOUND OF MANY BELLS and, BUILDING, THE SOUND OF GAL-LOPING HORSES. A body goes THROUGH FRAME, blocks our view. Another. Then another, BLURRING, streaking past.

107 WIDE ANGLE—DAY

Exploding over the hill, riding down on the damp, fifty Somali horsemen, wooden saddles, spears, swords. African Bedouins, cloaked and turbaned.

The camp bolts awake. The Kikuyu run for the wagon, some for the bush. Farah, Karen, and Ismail stare . . .

Then, suddenly bearing down on them: two white men! Denys and Berkeley, riding hard. Karen stares in shock. Berkeley reins up abruptly, Denys beside him, the horsemen behind them.

BERKELEY

What the devil are you doing out here?

KAREN

I'm on my way to Delamere.

FAST MOVE IN to Berkeley.

BERKELEY

Why?

108 CLOSE—DENYS ON HORSEBACK—DAY

Chin in hand, elbow on knee, legs crossed, assessing the argu-ment O.S.

56

This is ridiculous!

WIDEN to see the camp packed, oxen inspanned, final items being loaded. Berkeley stands, hands on hips, glaring at a resolute Karen, packing her bedroll.

> BERKELEY (continuing)
> We don't send women to a war! You're being pig-headed!
> (silence)
> Karen, we haven't time for this; you don't even know where you are!

> KAREN
> Yes I do . . . now.

> BERKELEY
> You'll just get lost again.

> KAREN
> I'm going on, Berkeley.

She mounts her horse. Berkeley turns to Denys:

> BERKELEY
> Talk to her, will you.

> DENYS
> No.

> BERKELEY
> (a moment)
> We'll go with her to Delamere then.

> DENYS
> What about Buxton? We're a day late already —suppose he's run onto the Germans?

> BERKELEY
> She could be hurt. Or worse.

> DENYS
> (nodding)
> I imagine she knows that.

Berkeley looks from Denys to Karen. A beat, then Denys dismounts, walks to her, takes a compass from his pocket, hands it up to her.

                    DENYS (continuing)
          Find a point on the horizon each morning and
          steer by it. South-southwest. About three days.

                         KAREN
          I see.

                         DENYS
                      (small grin)
          Don't worry about us—we'll be all right.

As he moves toward his horse:

                    DENYS (continuing)
          I'll want a story. A longer one this time.

109   EXT. PLAIN—DAY

OPEN ON herd of Thompson's gazelle. PAN TO Karen, elbows braced on knees, aiming her rifle. Ismail's optimistic, knife drawn; Juma's doubtful. Far in b.g. the ox wagon against the afternoon sun. The CRACK of Karen's RIFLE, and Ismail whoops off. Juma smiles.

110   EXT. CAMP—NIGHT

Around the FIRE: the six natives eating, joking in Swahili. PAN PAST their faces . . . and HOLD ON the Baroness von Blixen, face greasy with meat, squatting on her heels with them.

111   EXT. CAMP—CLOSE—COMPASS—MORNING

Sun GLINTS off it as we WATCH the needle swing. PULL BACK TO SEE Karen searching for a landmark.

112   KAREN'S P.O.V.—THE PLAIN—LONG SHOT—MORNING

Still, then, far off, an intermittent GLINT of sun on metal.

113 CLOSE—KAREN

Shading her eyes.

KAREN

Farah . . . ?

ANGLE ADJUSTS: Farah looks up, follows her gaze. He speaks sharply to Ismail in Swahili, who goes to the wagon for Karen's rifle. As Farah joins her:

KAREN (continuing)

What is it?

Quiet. All watch the horizon. Karen stands on the wagon box to see, looks at Farah. He's bleak:

FARAH

Masai.

114 EXTREMELY LONG LENS—MASAI—MORNING

Pulled together by the lens, appearing to run on water: a dozen young MASAI WARRIORS loping easily along, naked, slim spears SHINING in the sun.

115 EXT. CAMP—SERIES OF CUTS—DAY

A. A Kikuyu at the oxen, staring.

B. Karen, fingering her rifle.

C. Juma, hefting a panga.

116 THE MASAI—WIDE SHOT—DAY

Wildest of the wild. Carrying huge shields like feathers, penises tied to thighs with thongs. Some bleed slightly from thorn scratches. They cross no more than fifty yards ahead, hewing to their crow-flies line of march.

117 FULL SHOT—ALL—DAY

The Masai look at the camp as they pass, their manner bold, indifferent. One yips a wild SOUND. Silence . . . Then Karen relaxes, stares after them, curious.

118   EXT. BUSH COUNTRY—DAY

The terrain different now: whistling thorn and wait-a-bit.
Ostriches POUND the earth with big feet, scurrying out of the
way of the passing caravan.

119   EXT. CAMP—NIGHT

The thorn-bush corral (a boma) contains the restless oxen; a
Kikuyu CROONS to them. Dinner is over. Juma puts cooking
gear away. PUSH CLOSE TO SEE him move KAREN's rifle, shuffle
some boxes so that the rifle's inadvertently hidden. Notice a
stock whip.

120   THE SLEEPING CAMP—NIGHT

Around the EMBERS of campfire, the six sleeping natives and
Karen. Silence . . . Then the form of a lion moves through f.g.
. . . And again, stillness. O.S. a LOW GROWL, Karen's eyes open;
a beat, then the horrible SCREAM of an injured ox. SOUNDS of
oxen struggling, BAWLING. Karen runs for the wagon, SHOUTS
for Ismail.

121   ANGLE ON WAGON—NIGHT

She tears into it, searching frantically for her rifle. O.S. the
terrible NOISE from oxen. She snatches up the stock whip,
runs for the corral.

122   TRAVELING WITH KAREN—NIGHT

As she plunges through thorn bushes, ripping her clothes,
arms, face. SNARL of a lion as he flees past her. Inside the
corral another lion battles an ox. Ismail runs for Karen with
her rifle—but too late: she's at the lion with her whip. The
lion whirls, may come for her . . . But she's attacking! CRACK!
CRACK! CRACK! And Ismail, brave and distressed, runs at
the lion, swinging the rifle like a club!

The lion finally leaps the thorn barrier and runs off. Karen,
dazed, wipes her face, licks blood from her hand.

The ox, fatally mauled, BAWLS pathetically. Juma looks to
Karen, who nods. He reaches BELOW FRAME with his knife,
slits the ox's throat.

123 EXT. CAMPFIRE—FARAH AND KAREN—NIGHT

She sits on the ground, holding the back of her shirt up while
Farah treats deep scratches on her naked back.

> FARAH
> This simba thinks; tonight I must eat this ox.
> But msabu *speaks* to this simba: do not eat this ox
> or I can whip you with my little whip.

Karen, in pain, smiles nevertheless.

> FARAH (continuing)
> Now this simba is hungry in his own village. He
> says to all the wives: "Do not think to eat the
> oxes who pull this wagon. There is a memsaab
> there who is a witch."
> (he starts to laugh)
> Msabu is *bleeding*; *she* does not have this ox. This
> lion is hungry; he does not have this ox. This
> wagon is heavy; it does not have this ox.
> (beat)
> God is happy, msabu. He plays with us.

124 EXT. DELAMERE'S CAMP—DAY

Many tents. White men ride in, depart. Natives are busy at
chores, some female, a few quite beautiful. FEATURE Delamere
at a map-littered campaign desk. A man on horseback moves
to him, points. Delamere takes binoculars, stands up, moves
to look.

125 DELAMERE'S P.O.V.—KAREN AND CARAVAN

Approaching at a distance.

126 THE CAMP—DELAMERE—DAY

Lowering the binoculars. Beat, then:

> DELAMERE
> Tell Blix his wife is here.

127 KAREN'S ENTRANCE—HIGH ANGLE—DAY

CRANE DOWN as she enters camp. Men stop in their work to stare. Notice the HUGE MAN from the Muthaiga Club. Karen looks horrible; lips cracked, nose peeling, clothes torn, hair matted, infected scratches on her face and arms. But she feels fine. They are a tough bunch, and they don't say much, but they're impressed. At the end of their ragged line, Bror and Delamere.

                    DELAMERE
                     (quiet)
     Hello, Karen.

                     KAREN
     Hello, D. Hello, Bror. I've brought you some
     things.

                      BROR
     You've changed your hair.

She laughs. They don't.

128 INT. BROR'S TENT—KAREN AND BROR—NIGHT

In tied shorts. Gear strewn about. An old carpet.

                     KAREN
     You needed supplies!

                      BROR
     Send someone, I said! You were lucky to get
     through.
                      (then)
     It was foolish, Tanne.

                    KAREN [18]
     Bror, listen, you won't run from anything, you
     never have, that's how you know you're brave.
     Do you realize I could have lived all my life and
     never once been really at risk. It's absurd . . . I've
     assumed I was a coward; how would I know other-
     wise? It's not right the way we're kept safe.

She drinks. He remains silent. Her tone changes:

                       62

KAREN (continuing)
When are you coming home?

BROR
. . . Not just yet.

KAREN
(pause)
You're not going to help with the farm at all . . .
are you?

BROR
(with difficulty)
. . . No.

KAREN
I could force you. Cut you off.

BROR
(quietly)
I'd just hunt professionally.

KAREN
. . . Well . . .

BROR
I may do that, anyway.

KAREN
(beat)
It's not the way we thought, is it?
(then)
I like it that you're honest with me.

BROR
I like you too. Very much.

He moves to kiss her, his hands go under her shirt. PUSH TO
the lantern as her hand reaches out to extinguish it. HOLD ON
BLACKNESS. Then—

129 INT. BROR'S TENT—MORNING

Dressed, ready to leave, Karen stands over Bror, sleeping. A beat, then she bends to kiss his bare shoulder.

130   EXT. THE CAMP—HIGH ANGLE—MORNING

Gray dawn, the camp asleep, Karen walks alone down the rows of tents.

131   EXT. THE FARM—KIKUYU CHILDREN—DAY

Playing a pebble game in the dirt. PAN TO Karen, grimy, working on the pipes of an elevated cistern. She climbs down the ladder, steps to the ground, and her leg buckles. Puzzled, she takes a step, collapses like a doll, sitting. She's baffled; her legs aren't working.

132   INT. BEDROOM—KAREN AND FARAH—NIGHT

Kerosene lantern. She's wet with fever; he sits beside her. She gags; he wipes her mouth. She tries, clumsily, to push his hand away. He touches her forehead; knobby black fingers stroking her brow. She sighs, drifts away.

133   INT. DOCTOR'S OFFICE—DAY

Primitive equipment. The DOCTOR is forty to fifty, Irish. He pours two glasses of whiskey. Karen dresses behind a screen.

> DOCTOR
> You've got syphilis.

> KAREN'S VOICE
> . . . That's not possible.

> DOCTOR
> Your husband's not ill?

She steps out from behind the screen.

> KAREN
> Not the last I saw him . . . But that's three months.
> He's on the border with Delamere. But he'd've
> come home.

64

DOCTOR

Well . . . these cases vary; he may have just a
touch. You're quite ill.
(then)
Is he . . . the only possibility?

KAREN

Yes.

DOCTOR

You'll have to go home to deal with it. The
treatment's . . . difficult. They've got a thing
called Salvarsan—

KAREN
(grim)

Arsenic.
(then)
If I'm not cured, I'll be insane, won't I?

DOCTOR

You ought to go soon. I've have to see your
husband.

KAREN

I'll send for him.
(beat)
What are my chances?

DOCTOR

About even, I'm afraid.

She gathers up her things.

KAREN

It's not what I thought would happen to me now.

She goes to the door, turns:

KAREN (continuing)
If I live . . . and don't go mad . . . children?

DOCTOR
That wouldn't be wise. No.

134   EXT. DOCTOR'S OFFICE—NAIROBI—DAY

Farah waits by the wagon. Notice a few more automobiles, a few more buildings. Karen comes out, Farah helps her up into the wagon, concerned.

> FARAH
> Muthaiga, msabu?

> KAREN
> (distracted)
> . . . What . . . ?

> FARAH
> Your letters, msabu . . . ?

> KAREN
> . . . Oh . . . yes.

135   INT. MUTHAIGA CLUB—LOBBY—DAY

CLOSE ON a stack of mail as hands take it. PULL BACK TO SEE Karen at the desk. As she turns to go, Denys comes down the stairs with an ATTRACTIVE WOMAN. He excuses himself, moves to Karen, smiles.

> DENYS
> I *heard* you'd made it. I'd have paid to see that.

His friend moves to the doorway of the dining room, stands waiting, arms folded.

> KAREN
> It was just as you said: find a mark in the morning and make for it.

> DENYS
> Have a drink with us?

> KAREN
> I can't. How is it you're home?

> DENYS
> I've brought Berkeley back.

66

KAREN
(alarmed)
Has he been wounded?

DENYS
Fever . . . More than the usual. He'll be fine. As
long as the gin holds out.

KAREN
You? . . . You don't seem quite yourself.

He starts to protest, then, curiously, doesn't.

DENYS
(a smile)
We've taken a beating. It's got . . . real now.

KAREN
I've got your compass.

DENYS
Why don't you keep it . . . you've earned it.
(then)
I don't always like to know where I'm going,
anyway.

The woman waits quietly in the background.

KAREN
Please don't let me keep you.

DENYS
Is . . . everything all right?

KAREN
Take good care, Denys.

He notices she's used his first name.

DENYS
Thanks.
(then)
We're behind a story or two.

67

KAREN

Yes. When I get back.

DENYS

Back? From where?

KAREN

When *you* get back, I meant.

136 EXT. FRENCH MISSION HOSPITAL—DAY

In the garden, Karen stands with Kamante. A feeling of
goodbye.

BROR'S VOICE

. . . just a bit of fever. I thought it was malaria.

137 INT. LIVING ROOM—KAREN AND BROR—NIGHT

She's bundled up, withdrawn. He's sunburned and gaunt.
Dusk sits at her feet.

KAREN

Well, it wasn't. You may be all right, but you
have to be seen.
(beat)
The others, too. Whoever *they* may be . . . I hope
they've got it.

Bror is stricken, miserable.

BROR

It's my fault, Tanne, no one else's.

KAREN

God, you think so little of us we're not even
accessories.

BROR

I want to go with you.

KAREN

No. I want you to stay here. One of us has to run
things. Can you do that?

68

BROR
It's little enough.

KAREN
We've had bad luck, my friend. I don't know
how this will go. It's either shoot you or let it be;
time may improve your chances.

BROR
(low)
I'm terribly sorry, Tanne.

KAREN
. . . You might have a crop before I'm back . . .

138 EXT. HOUSE—FARAH—MORNING

Loading Karen's luggage onto the wagon. Several Kikuyu
hover or squat nearby, watching. Dusk is on the lawn. Bror
comes out of the house, looks at his watch.

BROR
Where is the memsaab?

FARAH
She can come soon enough.

Bror stares. Farah's gaze is cold, unafraid.

139 EXT. THE GROUNDS—KAREN—DAY

Standing under a tree, a shawl over her shoulder, she looks
out over the land. CAMERA PULLS AWAY until she is a tiny
figure, and we hear:

OLDER KAREN (V.O.)
Later that day I left for Mombasa and the voy-
age home to Denmark. It was a longer journey
this time:

140 MONTAGE

A NATIVE SONG OVER:

A. BLACK-AND-WHITE FILM, the fighting in France.

B. BEDROOM—KAREN'S VANITY: Combs, brushes, perfume, part of her empty bed in the mirror.

> OLDER KAREN (V.O.)
> The war in Europe went on. I fought my own war. Arsenic was my ally—against a corkscrew enemy I never saw.

C. BUSH COUNTRY—BERKELEY AND DENYS, unshaved, tired, ride through swampy marsh with bone-tired Somalis.

> OLDER KAREN (V.O.)
> I stayed in this room in Rungstedland and tried to remember the colors of Africa—but I looked out of a window that framed the cold essence of Denmark.

D. BEDROOM—KAREN'S VANITY: Combs, brushes, perfume. OUT OF FOCUS in the mirror, a woman undressing. Her pearls are dropped into f.g. in SHARP FOCUS.

E. LIVING ROOM—BROR working at the books; bored and listless. He goes to stare out the window.

F. SHAMBAS—RAIN falling hard, the huts and mud street deserted. One figure walking.

> OLDER KAREN (V.O.)
> There was only the medicine, and walks with my mother along a deserted stretch of beach . . . and this room.

G. BLACK-AND-WHITE FILM—The Americans enter the war. Doughboys boarding troop ships.

H. BEDROOM—KAREN'S VANITY. Farah carefully dusts her things. A photo of Karen and Bror:

> OLDER KAREN (V.O.)
> Denmark had become a stranger to me, and I to her. But the room . . . I came to know. And knew I'd come back to it, sick or well, sane or mad,

someday. And so I did. After Tsavo.

MUSIC FADES.

141 EXT. NAIROBI TRAIN STATION—BROR—DAY

Dusk beside him, he scans disembarking passengers, some military, some new settlers, baggage laden. MOVE IN to reveal Karen, older, gaunt, more beautiful. She looks around, opens her arms; it's the dog who leaps into them, nearly bowls her over.

142 ANOTHER ANGLE—KAREN AND BROR

As she sees him, hesitates, then moves to him. They hug. HOLD, then:

143 EXT. TRAIN STATION—MOTORCAR—DAY

Roofed, open. PULL BACK as Bror loads her carpetbags.

> BROR
> (apologetic)
> Most everyone's got them now.

144 TRAVELING SHOT—BROR AND KAREN—DAY

The car jounces along.

Bror occasionally glances over toward her. She watches the countryside, sees the new power lines. After a beat:

> BROR
> They say we'll have telephones in a year.

PAN OFF her, to see the African countryside.

145 EXT. THE HOUSE—DAY

She descends into a clutch of Kikuyu. Much BABBLE. One old woman pinches her arm, clucks disapproval. The Cuckoo Clock Child hands her a baby owl. She accepts, says, "Asante." Overcome, he runs away.

146 EXT. VERANDA—DAY

Kamante, older now, leg wrapped in old bandages, feigns a
limp, then, with great effect, unwraps his left, scarred but
well. Karen is delighted.

> KAMANTE
> I am cooking now, memsaab.

> KAREN
> We'll see about that.

She touches his shoulder, but her eyes are for Farah. She
strokes the owl, moves to Farah. A beat.

> KAREN (continuing)
> Are you well, Farah Aden?

> FARAH
> I am well enough, msabu.

> KAREN
> Then I am well enough also.

147 INT. BEDROOM—KAREN AND BROR—NIGHT

OPEN ON a new electric lamp. PULL BACK TO SEE them getting
ready for bed. They both have brandy; the baby owl eats off a
paper on the vanity. An air of formality, perhaps tension.

> KAREN
> (quietly)
> What will you do?

> BROR
> (a pause)
> I've been thinking I'll hunt. The safari sort of
> thing. They say it'll be quite a business once the
> war is over.

> KAREN
> (nods, then wryly)
> . . . You wouldn't like to teach, would you?
> (at his look)
> I want my Kikuyu to have a school.

                    BROR
        There'll be a fight about that . . .
                (then, carefully)
        Are you *all* well, Tanne?

                    KAREN
        Physically I'm cured. I won't have children.

                    BROR
        . . . Have you thought about us?

                    KAREN
        Of course . . .

Silence. She removes a bracelet, places it on the vanity. PAN
with her hand, HOLD ON them in the mirror.

                    BROR
                (beat; then quietly)
        Belknap says the coffee'll flower after the next
        rains. If it does, you'll have to start thinking
        about hiring for the harvest. And how you'll get
        to market . . .

During above, CAMERA MOVES from the mirror and FINDS Finch
Hatton's compass beside her comb on the vanity.

148/149   OMITTED

150   EXT. HOUSE—MOTORCAR—DAY

    Karen gets in, examines the controls, nods to Farah at the
    crank. Natives watch, grave. The ENGINE SPUTTERS, ROARS.
    Farah weighs the odds, reluctantly gets in.

                    KAREN
        You don't have to, Farah.

                    FARAH
        God is great, msabu.

The car CLANKS into gear, bucks away across the lawn. SOUNDS
OF RAGGED MARTIAL MUSIC.

150a EXT. NAIROBI STREET—NIGHT

Native troops, carring TORCHES, march through the streets. An Indian MILITARY BAND PLAYS. Settlers and natives drink, sing, celebrate, FIRE PISTOLS. An occasional burst of FIREWORKS. A "Victory" sign or two.

FIND Karen and Bror moving through the happy crowd, Bror obviously popular, being waved at by an occasional attractive woman. Karen is looking around.

> KAREN
> Where would Berkeley be?

> BROR
> He must be back.

Coming the other direction, a group of friends. Bror stops to chat, Karen smiles but keeps moving, searching the parade of people.

> DENYS'S VOICE
> Have you got a story for me?

She turns, sees him leaning against a post, slightly drunk. He's in uniform, shirt open, holds a bottle of champagne.

> KAREN
> Finch-Hatton!

> DENYS
> I've been demoted—I was Denys last time.
> (beat between them)
> Some champagne?

She shakes her head no.

> DENYS (continuing)
> They said you went home for a while.

> KAREN
> Yes.
> (barely a beat)
> Where's Berkeley?

DENYS
It's good to see you, Karen.

She looks at him a beat—he looks back to the parade.

DENYS (continuing)
He's still down with fever. He'll be all right—
(gesturing)
—Who *are* all these people?

Karen turns to look. The people file by. Then:

KAREN
Bror says we'll be a colony soon.

DENYS
(an edge)
They want it settled now: They've got a lottery
—"Buy a ticket, win a farm in Africa."

KAREN
. . . Did you really think everything would stay as
it was?

DENYS
(knows better, but)
. . . Yes . . . I did.

She smiles sympathetically. A group of black K.A.R. march by,
led by a white officer.

KAREN
Where's Kanuthia?

DENYS
. . . Dead.

Karen reacts as Bror joins them.

BROR
Hello, Denys! . . . Who's dead?

KAREN
Kanuthia.

BROR[19]
(not unkindly)
Oh, yes, I remember now . . . Reliable, wasn't
he? I could use one like that. Come—

DENYS
—One what?—

BROR
—join us for a drink—

DENYS
—They were all fools. Recruited in a language
they didn't understand, paid with things they
didn't need—to fight for a place that was theirs
to begin with.

BROR
—What're you talking about?

BROR
Why didn't he know better?—

BROR
—Who?

DENYS
—You know what turned the trick? I told him
he was needed . . . and he believed me.

BROR
(gently)
Denys . . . You're drunk.

DENYS
No.
(then)
I just . . . knew better.

Silence. Bror's taken none of it personally.

BROR
Come on . . . join us for a drink.

"The notion of beginning as though Karen is going back in time to reexamine Denys was intended to suggest memory, establish a rhythm and pace, and dictate a kind of style."—Sydney Pollack, from the Introduction. PHOTOS BY FRANK CONNOR.

Karen and Bror in Denmark (left) and in Africa on their wedding day (below). (Opposite page) Karen is stunned by Bror's departure the day after her arrival, and turns to helping "her Kikuyu" Kamante while Farah looks on. PHOTOS BY FRANK CONNOR.

Possession. Freedom versus obligation. That was Pollack's "spine" or "armature." "Trivial as it may sound," he writes, "it's important to me to be able to describe the heart of a film simply and evocatively in order to test each scene, character, development against that idea." PHOTOS BY FRANK CONNOR.

BLIXEN

MOMBASA

NAIROBI

Stubbornly independent, Karen works with the natives in the Kikuyu village (top) and arrives at Lord Delamere's camp after a grueling and dangerous journey (bottom). PHOTOS BY FRANK CONNOR.

"Denys Finch Hatton's charm covered a terror of emotional commitment, and Redford understands this. He knows how to show the loneliness of a man everyone loves."—David Ansen, *Newsweek*. PHOTOS BY FRANK CONNOR.

After Karen's reading of the eulogy, screenwriter Luedtke created the *Lions on the Grave Monologue* ("The mail has come today, and a friend writes this to me . . .") partly from Dinesen's book, but the framework and large sections of it had to be invented. PHOTOS BY FRANK CONNOR.

DENYS
(shaking head)
Time to find a pillow.

KAREN
Another night, then.

He looks at her. As she and Bror start off:

KAREN (continuing)
Have a good Christmas.

DENYS
Christmas?
(then)
So it is.

But she's gone.

150b EXT. COFFEE FIELDS—WIDE—DAY

A rolling sea of white blossoms on green leaves, rich with promise. Karen and Belknap walk among them, Karen smiling with excitement. MUSIC.

151 EXT. GROUNDS—MAKESHIFT SCHOOLHOUSE—DAY

A thatched roof on posts over bare earth. BEGIN CLOSE on a post as a machete WHACKS into it, cutting a notch about three and one-half feet above the ground. ADJUST TO SEE Kinanjui, Karen and Farah, native workers in b.g. Kinanjui speaks vehemently in Swahili.

FARAH
This chief says children higher than this . . .
(indicates)
. . . must not learn to read.

KAREN
Tell him *all* the children must go to school.

FARAH
No, msabu. This is a chief. You are not a chief.

77

She turns to argue, but Kinanjui has already walked off. She turns back to Farah.

                    KAREN
          That's absurd.

                    FARAH
          It is not good for tall people to know more than
          this chief. When these totos are tall, then this
          chief can be dead.

152   EXT. MUTHAIGA CLUB—WIDE—NIGHT

The lights and DISTANT SOUNDS OF MUSIC AND PARTY. Natives in kanzus slosh paraffin at the base of a twenty-foot pyramid of cordwood.

153   INT. MUTHAIGA CLUB—NIGHT

New Years's Eve, jammed with settlers in evening clothes. Some NEW FACES, loud, pushy. MOVE THROUGH TO SEE Bror flirting with a NEW ARRIVAL. Karen and Berkeley, a few others dance to the INDIAN TRIO.

                    KAREN
          —Bror, yes, but *Denys* hired out to tourists . . . ?

                    BERKELEY
          It's the only trade he's got. In any case, he's got
          no choice—government's put a stop to the ivory.

                    FELICITY'S VOICE
          Hello the house!

WIDEN TO REVEAL FELICITY, a young woman now, dancing with an older man. Both couples continue dancing.

                    KAREN
          Why are you home?

                    FELICITY
          I'm out! Look!

She shows off her fingernails, painted, immaculate.

78

FELICITY (continuing)
Didn't learn a thing, but I'm wonderfully clean.
I'll come see you—save me a dance, Berkeley.

She dances away.

KAREN
Yesterday she was twelve.

The dance ends, SCATTERED APPLAUSE. FOLLOW Karen and
Berkeley to the open bar, where they wait with Delamere,
others, among them a BEEFY DRUNK who'll overhear.

DELAMERE
Karen. What's this nonsense I hear about a school?

KAREN
I've taken on a young missionary. I want them to
learn to read.

DELAMERE
Good Lord.

BEEFY DRUNK
Wogs can't even count their goats. None of your
bloody business, anyway.

BERKELEY
Just who the devil are you?

The Drunk shoves Berkeley, staggers him. Karen slaps the
Drunk. Delamere grabs the Drunk. Denys steps INTO SHOT,
takes Karen's arm.

DENYS
I wonder if you'd dance with me.

He leads her OUT OF THE SHOT.

DELAMERE
(to Drunk)
I believe you're about to apologize.

79

154 THE DANCE FLOOR—KAREN AND DENYS—NIGHT

He takes her hand and they begin dancing. A beat.

> DENYS[20]
> You're an awful lot of trouble, Baroness.
> (pause)
> When they said they wanted to read, how did
> they put that, exactly? I mean, do they *know*
> they'll like Dickens?
> (no response)
> It's just . . . shouldn't you have asked them?

> KAREN
> (a look, before)
> Is life really so damned easy for you, Finch-
> Hatton?

> DENYS
> (shrugs)
> I ask less of it than you do.

> KAREN
> . . . I don't believe that at all.

O.S. CRIES of Happy New Year! The Trio stops mid-song.
Denys and Karen stop dancing. The thin beginnings of "Auld
Lang Syne."

155 EXT. THE LAWN—NIGHT[21]

People begin spilling out. Delamere sets a torch to the wood-
pile; it catches quickly. In the b.g.: Bror and the attractive
woman MOVE THROUGH SHOT, going off.

156 INT. CLUB—KAREN AND DENYS—NIGHT

Karen looks around for Bror, then back to Denys, awkward.
They are the only ones not kissing. Denys feels her discomfort;
she doesn't know what to do. SOUND OF A SHOT, O.S. They
turn.

156a EXT. THE LAWN—BONFIRE—NIGHT[22]

A DOWAGER has taken a revolver from her purse, FIRES A SECOND SHOT now. A hush.

156b INT. CLUB—KAREN AND DENYS

A mix of relief and regret as "Auld Lang Syne" ends.

> DENYS
>
> Happy New Year.

> KAREN
>
> Yes, for you, too.

She moves away. As the dowager, in a quavering voice, begins to SING "God Save the King." The settlers join in. Flawed, dissolute, but loving their country, far from home.

158/159 OMITTED

160 EXT. THE BLIXENS' CAR—BROR AND WOMAN—NIGHT[23]

He seems to open his trousers, shielded by her: she fumbles beneath her long dress; we think she's removed her panties. She sits astride him, drops the straps of her dress.

161 EXT. THE EYES OF AN IMPALA—NIGHT[24]

Reflecting the lights of an oncoming car. The animal bounds out of the way as the car passes.

162 INT. THE BLIXEN'S CAR—KAREN AND BROR—NIGHT

Bror driving. They ride in silence. Then:

> KAREN
>
> Someone's left her underclothes in back.

A long silence.

> KAREN (continuing)
>
> I'd like you to take a place in town.

Again, silence. Then:

81

BROR
Are you sure, Tanne?

She does not answer. The silent ride continues.

163   INT. DRAWING ROOM—GUN RACK—DAY

Empty except for her rifle. Her hand wanders over the empty slot. WIDEN to see her staring at it a moment. She turns, sees herself in the mirror. She grabs a hat, goes out.

164   EXT. SCHOOLHOUSE—DAY

A dozen small Kikuyu children sit on the ground, facing a YOUNG MAN in horn-rimmed glasses who holds up a picture book. Karen trudges past, walking as though she's determined to exhaust herself.

165   EXT. KIKUYU SHAMBAS—KAREN—DAY

Old woman calls: "Jambo, Jerie," but she doesn't respond. A young Kikuyu mother sits at the door of her hut, nursing her baby. Karen notices, keeps moving determinedly.

166   WIDE ANGLE—COFFEE FIELDS—DAY

The Kikuyu picking, stripping red berries, filling wooden baskets. Karen's figure moves purposefully through the coffee trees.

167   EXT. COFFEE SHED AND FACTORY—DAY

Pickers dump their baskets, add to a huge pile of berries. As they pass, Belknap drops a coin in the empty baskets. The workers separate as Karen approaches, stops before Belknap.

KAREN
Give me work.

168   EXT. DRYING TABLES—KAREN AND KIKUYU WOMEN—DAY

Husked beans dumped in mounds on long tables. They must be spread thin, evenly, the bottom beans churned to the top. Hot, robotic work. She's joined the line of native women, who watch her, keep their distance.

169   EXT. COFFEE SHED—NIGHT

Kerosene lamps. With male Kikuyu, she shovels dried beans
into huge burlap sacks. She's sweat-soaked, haggard.

170   INT. DINING ROOM—FARAH—NIGHT

Arms folded, silent, watchful. FOLLOW his gaze to find Karen,
head on arms, asleep at the table, her dinner unfinished.
HOLD. Then:

171   EXT. COFFEE SHED—KAREN AND BELKNAP—DAY

An ox wagon loaded with sacked coffee, drivers ready to go.
Belknap has a grimy ledger.

> KAREN
> We've got peace—where's the prosperity? Why
> should prices fall *now*? Just because we're not
> killing anyone?

> BELKNAP
> Tea's down just as bad.

The wagon moves out, the drivers' WHIPS CRACKING.

> KAREN
> Do they always have to whip them so?

172   EXT. DRIVEWAY—KAREN—DAY

Walking back under the jacaranda trees. A different Karen
from the woman who came to Africa. Now, faint, O.S. the
SOUND OF SYMPHONIC MUSIC. She hears it, is perplexed, quick-
ens her stride.

173   EXT. TERRACE—DENYS—DAY

A new gramophone plays MOZART. Juma rolls out drink cart.
PAN AROUND to see Karen approaching, past Denys's parked
safari truck. Natives stare, glare.

DENYS

Look here: They've finally made a machine that's really useful.

She doesn't respond.

DENYS (continuing)

It's for you.

KAREN

I can't accept it.

DENYS

Why not?

KAREN

Because Bror's moved to town.

DENYS

That's a private matter, I imagine.

KAREN
(beat, even)
Did you think you'd spend the night?

DENYS

Can't, thanks.
(beat)
I'm going up to the Aberdares. I've taken up safari work; I've got to find a camp.

KAREN
(long pause)
No . . .

DENYS

There's country there you ought to see. It won't last long now.

KAREN [25]

I'd be wasting your time; I won't sleep with you.

DENYS

You'll do as you like.

84

(then)

Why don't you just jump the fence? Wait to see what happens.

KAREN

I can't afford much, right now.

DENYS
(beat)

Life's not years, Karen. It's just a day here and a minute there—a few fine moments. You've got to collect them.

KAREN

If you like me at all, don't ask me to do this.

DENYS[26]
(quiet)

All right.

In profile, they look at one another across some distance. HOLD their figures. Then a . . .

SLOW DISSOLVE TO:

174 LONG VIEW—OPEN PLAIN—SAFARI TRUCK—DAY

Moving toward us, between the fading images of Karen and Denys. Three natives are in back, Karen and Denys in front.

175 INT. TRUCK—KAREN AND DENYS—TRAVELING—DAY

She's stiff, pinched, certain she shouldn't have come.

176 EXT. GRASSY RANGE—ZEBRA—DAY

A large herd, grazing. A few raise their heads. PAN AROUND to see the safari truck approaching.

177 INT. TRUCK—KAREN AND DENYS—DAY

A beat. Denys inclines his head toward the zebra.

85

DENYS
White on black or black on white—which do you think?

She doesn't respond. Then she shifts her gaze to the zebra. A beat, then, musing:

DENYS (continuing)[27]
There's a reason for those stripes. Or was. But I can't make it work. It doesn't hide them. Unless . . . this was all light and shadow once.
(beat)
We ought to ask the lions, they're the ones who'd know.

A beat. She shifts her gaze to Denys. He drives.

177a EXT. GRASSLAND—TRUCK—DAY

The lorry works its way through a herd of Cape buffalo. A massive bull glares, baleful and murderous. The engine COUGHS, SPUTTERS, DIES. They've broken down in the midst of the herd. A quiet moment, then:

DENYS
What's your word?
(to the buffalo)
Shoo!—Shoo!

First the nearest animals, then the herd, wheel and jog away.

DENYS (continuing)
That's a fine word you've got there, Baroness.

178 EXT. GRASSLAND—LATER—DAY

The truck's hood is open. Denys leans in from the side, tinkers with a screwdriver. Karen and three natives watch from the front.

DENYS
(not looking up)
Crank it, will you.

Karen glances at the natives. Nobody moves. She moves uncertainly forward, cranks it. A SPUTTER. He adjusts, says: Again. A SPUTTER. Adjusts. Again. A SPUTTER. Adjusts. Again. The ENGINE COMES ALIVE.

He closes the hood, pleased with himself. Karen is out of breath.

179 EXT. THE ABERDARE FOOTHILLS—SUNSET

The beginnings of forest. Green, more lush. The truck labors through the trackless country.

180 EXT. FIRST NIGHT CAMP—DENYS AND KAREN—NIGHT

The tent's lantern lit. Two fires. Kerosene lamps on the white cloth table, the night pitch-black around the camp. Wine in a tin bucket of water. They're finishing their meal, Karen still withdrawn.

DENYS[28]
—only *men* do it badly sometimes, tire of going through it. The animals never take shortcuts. It's always fresh, full. And it's always for the first time. Only men say: See here, we've known each other for years, you know how I feel about you, why don't we lie down and get it over with?

They are silent for a moment. It's broken by an exchange in Swahili and a burst of LAUGHTER from the natives. Karen turns toward them, then curious, back to Denys.

DENYS (continuing)
It's about the tents. When I'm out with Kanuthia . . . *used* to be . . . I didn't use them.

A pause.

KAREN
What did the two of you ever find to talk about?

DENYS
. . . Nothing.

She looks at the two tents, the tablecloth, wine.

87

KAREN
So . . . You knew I'd come.

He returns her gaze but lets her question stand. It's clear in
any case. A beat of silence, then:

DENYS
It's an early day tomorrow; why don't you get
some sleep?

She nods, rises.

KAREN
What happens tomorrow?

DENYS
(cheerfully)
I have no idea.

KAREN
. . . Good night.

DENYS
Good night, Karen.

She goes to her tent. Denys takes a book out of his jacket,
opens it, picks up an orange. The NIGHT SOUNDS are louder.
Her movements cast shadows on the tent wall. Engrossed, he
ignores both the sounds and the shadows.

181/182   EXT. THE ABERDARES—SUNRISE

A magnificent sky, jagged hills sloping down toward CAMERA.
Across f.g. warthogs trot single file, brisk burghers on business.
The safari truck works its way through.

183   INT. TRUCK—KAREN AND DENYS—TRAVELING—DAY

They ride in silence.

183a EXT. A GLADE—CLOSE—GRAMOPHONE—DAY

Solitary under a tree, arm and needle on the unmoving record.
Beyond, we see baboons browsing in the glade.

A string is attached to the off-on switch! CAMERA FOLLOWS the string up to a low-hanging branch, then horizontally into the bush, beyond which, the staring faces of Karen and Denys.

183b WIDER ANGLE—THE GLADE—DAY

Suddenly the string is pulled, and MUSIC fills the glade! The baboons react: some peer, two come warily to the gramophone, study it.

183c KAREN AND DENYS

She's forgot her wariness. Very quietly:

KAREN
You'd think they'd run off.

DENYS
You didn't.

183d THE BABOONS

One brave fellow warily touches the machine, SCRATCHES the record.

183e WIDER ANGLE—THE GLADE, KAREN AND DENYS—DAY

Denys charges out of the bush.

DENYS
Hey!

The baboons scamper off, Karen emerges from the bush.

DENYS (continuing)
Think of that: never a manmade sound, and then . . . Mozart.

184 EXT. A RIVER—HIGH ANGLE—DAY[29]

A mirrored ribbon sparkling in the sun, belted with greenery. PULL UP TO HOLD Karen staring down at it. Denys moves up beside her.

DENYS

If I were a rich tourist with a brand-new gun,
that's where *I'd* want to camp. If I could get
down there . . .

KAREN

Have you clients already?

DENYS

In a week. A man from Belgium and his daugh-
ters. His letter said: We'd like three of everything.
(then)
Be an interesting trip: I'll be gone a month—or
an hour and a half.

KAREN

Why are you doing this?

DENYS
(shrugs)
I don't know how to sew.

O.S. A DRONING SOUND. He looks up.

184a P.O.V.—ANGLE ON PLANE—DAY

Solitary, brave, above them.

184b KAREN AND DENYS

Staring up, Denys with awe.

DENYS

D'you know what they're made of? . . . Cloth!

KAREN

Where will he land?

DENYS
(still gazing up)
The trick is not to.

Then, as he gets into the truck:

90

DENYS (continuing)
It must feel . . . amazing.

184c EXT. RIVER CAMP—WIDE—DAY

Denys and the three natives midway through setting up camp.
Karen now moves forward and begins to work along with
them. Denys brings a box from the lorry, sets it down. They
work side by side a moment.

KAREN
It's like America.

DENYS
Not really.

KAREN
. . . No.

DENYS
You've been to America?

KAREN
My father took me camping there when I was
little.

DENYS
Are you still close?

KAREN
(matter-of-factly)
He died. He killed himself. When I was twelve.

They continue to work in silence.

184d EXT. RIVER CAMP—KAREN—DAY

Her feet in the water, she sits on the bank, trying to get a
comb through her tangled hair. In b.g. Denys is making a
map. She gets up, moves toward the camp table, trying to
desnag her hair. Denys observes her a moment. Then:

DENYS
I can fix that, I think.

She's on a camp stool, in shorts and camisole, a towel around her shoulders. He's shirtless, suds to the elbows, having a fine time, reciting all the while.

> DENYS
>
> "—Laughed loud and long, and all the while
> His eyes went to and fro.
> Ha, ha, quoth he, full plain I see
> The Devil knows how to row.
>
> Farewell, farewell—"

> KAREN
>
> You're skipping verses.

> DENYS
>
> I leave out the dull parts:
> "Farewell, farewell, but this I tell
> To thee, thou Wedding Guest:
> He prayeth well, who loveth well
> Both man and bird and beast."

Pouring slowly, he rinses her hair. When she opens her eyes, he's looking at her.

> DENYS (continuing)
>
> That's better.

185/186   OMITTED

187/188   EXT. RIVER CAMP—CLOSE—WINE BOTTLE—NIGHT

PULL BACK to see Karen and Denys at the table, dinner finished, deep into their second bottle of wine. As the natives clear plates, Karen holds her glass for Denys to fill.

> KAREN[30]
>
> He'd be a fool not to love it here—your rich Belgian.

NIGHT SOUNDS. They are both on the way to being drunk.

DENYS

Listen. There's a thousand eyes out there—some of them people's—who don't want a glass of wine—

KAREN
(drinking)
That comes to five hundred animals . . . or people.

DENYS
(going on)
—and don't give a damn if we make it through the night.

KAREN
I find that . . . reassuring.

DENYS
It was meant to be.

Long pause.

KAREN
. . . Why am I here?

DENYS
I wanted you to see all this.
(he looks out)
It was kept safe a million years because we couldn't get here. When it's gone, we'll have no proof that there's another way.
(then)
What's useful here is that you can still see . . . what the intention was.

She thinks a moment. Then:

KAREN
Will it be so different, hunting for hire?

DENYS
Not for the animals, I suppose.
(drinks)
Maybe for the animals.

A Kikuyu native clears the last plate, leaves.

>   DENYS (continuing)[31]
> Notice how rarely one meets a Kikuyu building
> a shamba in Trafalgar Square?
>   (he looks up)
> There's the Pleiades . . . and that's Aldebaran.
>   (then)
> They've told us we can live forever. Used it for
> bait.

>   KAREN
> . . . Do you think much about dying?

>   DENYS
> I think about getting old.
>   (then)
> It'd be like living with a cranky, demanding old
> bastard.

>   KAREN
>   (quietly)
> You *are* a cranky, demanding old bastard.

A moment, the NIGHT SOUNDS PERSIST. Then:

>   KAREN (continuing)
> I had syphilis.
>   (then)
> That's why I went home.

Denys sips his wine. He nods.

>   DENYS
> I never seem to get anything. German measles,
> once.

A pause.

>   KAREN
> They say I'll have a normal life now. But no
> children.

94

DENYS
... So ... the school.

KAREN
I suppose.
(then)
We want to think we matter. That if we do it
well, there'll be something left behind.
(then)
The school—the farm ... that's what I am now.

DENYS
(long pause)
No.

She draws herself up against the chill of the night air. Denys
rises.

DENYS (continuing)
I'll get you a jacket.

He LEAVES FRAME. HOLD ON her, study her, until he returns.
Behind her, he places her jacket over her shoulders.

DENYS (continuing)
Don't wander off—there're lions.

He moves away slowly.

189 EXT. THE PLAIN—HUNTING SEQUENCE—DAY

A. DAWN: Karen checks a heavy rifle.

B. A TRACKER, Denys and Karen leave camp, their shadows
long against the rising sun.

C. A BROAD PLAIN: The three of them walking.

D. THIGH-HIGH GRASS: Karen walking through, beginning
to sweat, checking her rifle over and over.

E. IN DEEP BUSH: they're crouched, very still, looking off
toward a tree. Something under it. They wait.

F.   THE TREE: an animal gets up, *not* a lion, moves away.

G.   Denys shakes his head; they start away.

H.   WALKING under relentless sun.

I.   LUNCH: they squat. Denys eats a sandwich, gulps water. Karen's shirt is soaked with sweat. The tracker doesn't eat.

> DENYS
> It's like this some days.

J.   TRACKING. The sun beats down.

K.   WAITING, the three crouched close together.

> DENYS'S VOICE
> Everything gently, no sudden movements. Concentrate.

L.   LIONS: feeding on a zebra carcass. A large male among the lions.

M.   Denys, Karen and the tracker, on all fours. CAMERA CIRCLES: see the strain of holding still.

> DENYS'S VOICE
> They are very quick. I'll be behind you. If there's a charge, drop flat and let me do it.

N.   LIONS: eating.

O.   Denys with binoculars, his body close to Karen's. He carefully lowers glasses, nods.

P.   They rise, so-o-o-o slowly, move forward. Karen fingers the safety. Denys places extra cartridges between third and fourth fingers of his left hand.

> DENYS'S VOICE
> They snarl just before they come. It's to freeze you. Don't let it.

Q.   THE LIONS: the big male raises his head, sees them.

R.   Karen looks to Denys; he nods. She moves, Denys on her right, tracker on Denys's right.

S.   LIONS: about forty yards away now. The male steps forward.

T.   Karen raises rifle—but the SNARL is off to her left! ZOOM to her as she turns to Denys. FREEZE it.

U.   SLOW MOTION: on Karen's left, a LION explodes from the grass, charges for her. We see two bounds.

V.   SLOW MOTION: Denys turns, brings up his rifle.

W.   DENYS'S P.O.V.: Karen's squarely in his line of fire.

X.   VERY SLOW MOTION: Karen turns, smooth, the rifle easing onto her shoulder. We see it kick once, then again, silently. Only now do we hear the SHOT. AGAIN.

Y.   NORMAL SPEED: the lion stumbles, falls.

Z.   SLOW MOTION: the first big male charges, great leaps.

AA.   SLOW MOTION: Denys pivots, fires, the SOUND DELAYED.

BB.   SLOW MOTION: cordite smoke drifts in the air.

CC.   REAL TIME:

                         DENYS
        Load. Now.

Karen hastily tries to reload. Denys watches both fallen lions, back and forth. Tracker moves forward, throws stones at Karen's lion. It is dead. Denys checks his. Dead also.

190   CLOSER—KAREN

She hasn't moved. She's bit her lip, badly. Denys walks to her, nods slowly, approvingly. He notes blood, hands her his handkerchief.

97

190a EXT. THE RIVER—KAREN—SUNSET

It's green, idyllic, the light gone gold. She is at the river edge, cupping water to lave her arms and legs, soothe her lip. Denys comes INTO FRAME behind her, watches. Not startled, she turns to see him. A moment, then:

> DENYS
> Dinner in a while.
> (beat)
> I'm glad you came.

191 EXT. RIVER CAMP—NIGHT

The gramophone player on the ground. Denys, in a clean shirt, starts a record.

> DENYS
> (calling)
> Bar's open.

Karen comes from her tent. She's without makeup or jewelry, her hair drawn back with a ribbon. She's stunning. They look at one another a moment.

191a MONTAGE—GRAMOPHONE MUSIC OVER

A. Denys uncorks the wine, pours it. A silent toast.

B. As they eat, she's animated. He's intent on her. She stops talking, looks at him, addresses her food.

C. After dinner. Denys stands at the camp table, pours another glass. FOLLOW his gaze to FIND Karen at the edge of the firelight, looking out over the plain.

D. Karen kneels to wind the gramophone, start the record again.

E. One Kikuyu stands silent, watching. ANGLE ADJUSTS to see Karen and Denys in the b.g., dancing.

191b EXT. THE CAMPFIRE—NIGHT (LATER)

He pours the last of the wine into their tin cups.

> DENYS
> (a toast)
> Rose-lipt maidens.

NIGHT SOUNDS. The low CRACKLE of the FIRE.

> KAREN
> Is it Sunday tomorrow?

> DENYS
> Umm.
> (beat)
> We could stay another day.

> KAREN
> I ought to get back. The farm . . .[32]

> DENYS
> Yes.
> (beat)
> There was a very young girl from Denmark. Who
> took passage on a steamer. Bound for Suez . . .

> KAREN
> (vague)
> . . . There was a storm. Off Morocco. She was . . .
> washed ashore, on a beach . . . on a white beach
> . . . on a beach so white it . . .

She can't hold the thought, stares into the fire. She puts her
cup carefully on the table, stands. As she goes toward her tent,
she pauses just a moment to stand beside him. She touches
his shoulder, not looking at him. He doesn't watch as she
walks slowly on.

192 INT. HER TENT—KAREN—NIGHT

Unfastening the ties of her bodice when:

> DENYS (O.S.)
> I'd like to do that.

99

She turns, drops her arms like a schoolgirl. He moves INTO FRAME, unties the laces; with a forefinger slips a strap from her shoulder; very lightly touches her lip.

                    DENYS (continuing)
    Will that hurt?

She shakes her head: no. Ever so gently, he kisses her.

                    KAREN
    If you say anything, I'll believe it—I'm like that.

193 EXT. OPEN PLAIN—SAFARI TRUCK—DAY

Heading home through the long afternoon shadows.

193a INT. THE TRUCK—KAREN AND DENYS—AFTERNOON

They ride in silence a moment.

                    KAREN
    I need to know how to think about this.

                    DENYS
    . . . Why?

Silence. Then:

                    KAREN[33]
    You're like . . . a sketch someone drew very
    quickly.
                    (modifying it)
    A sketch *you* drew very quickly.

194 EXT. DRIVEWAY—KAREN'S FARM—SUNSET

The safari truck pulls up, stops. The natives jump out, hand her bags and the burlap-wrapped lion skin to Farah and Juma, who've come out of the house.

Denys moves around the truck to her side, but she has moved directly to the rear of the truck and taken the gramophone in her arms. He smiles as she approaches, raises his hand, touches her puffed lip.

100

She moves to the house, placing her hand on a toddler who clutches at her. She doesn't look back.

195 INT. KITCHEN—CLOSE—EGG WHITES—DAY

Being beaten by a rusty fork in Kamante's dexterous hands. See Karen's hands take the fork away, put an eggbeater in his hand. PULL BACK TO WIDE VIEW.

> KAREN
> Your clear soup. The new lettuce. Chicken. Just the breasts.
> (no response)
> I trust this has your approval?

> KAMANTE
> Who is coming, memsaab?

> KAREN
> Bwana Cole is coming.

> KAMANTE
> I will think on Bwana Cole.

Exasperated, she goes off. Kamante discards the eggbeater, returns to his rusty fork.

196 EXT. THE TERRACE—KIKUYU—NIGHT

Stand, squat, listening to O.S. GRAMOPHONE MUSIC.

197 INT. DINING ROOM—BERKELEY AND KAREN—NIGHT

In evening clothes. Berkeley perspires heavily.

> BERKELEY
> —so D. sent a runner. Took three days; "Urgent! Must reach George Grant; do you know his where-abouts?" I sent the runner back: "Yes."

They laugh. She quiets, sighs, lays down her fork:

> KAREN
> I've got myself in *real* trouble, Berkeley.

101

                    BERKELEY
Let's see . . . now you think they ought to vote.

                    KAREN
. . . Worse.

PUSH CLOSE to Berkeley's face as it dawns.

                    BERKELEY
. . . Denys.

She suddenly looks up from her plate, turns to Juma:

                    KAREN
Get Kamante.
                    (to Berkeley)
He's out of hand entirely.

She waits. Berkeley is still. When Kamante comes:

                    KAREN (continuing)
Does this look like chicken?

Kamante gravely inspects her plate, then:

                    KAMANTE
Here is not a chicken, memsaab. Here is a fish.

                    KAREN
Go away.

He does. A pause. Then Karen turns to Berkeley.

                    KAREN (continuing)
What do you think?

                    BERKELEY
                    (refers to food)
Quite good, isn't it?

                    KAREN
. . . Berkeley.

                    102

> BERKELEY
>
> . . . Be careful, Karen.
>> (a beat)
> When the old mapmakers got to the edge of the world, they'd write: "Beyond this place there be dragons."

> KAREN
>
> Is that where I am?
>> (then)
> He hasn't even said he'll come again.

> BERKELEY
>
> Would you divorce?

> KAREN
>
> . . . Then I'd have no one.

HOLD on his stricken face.

197a INT. DRAWING ROOM—KAREN AND FARAH—NIGHT[34]

She reads aloud. Farah dusts and arranges her desktop.

> KAREN
>
> "With rue my heart is laden
> For golden friends I had,
> For many a rose-lipt maiden
> And many a lightfoot lad."

> FARAH
>
> What is this about, msabu?

> KAREN
>> (a pause)
> "By brooks too broad for leaping
> The lightfoot boys are laid.
> The rose-lipt girls are sleeping
> In fields where roses fade."
>> (then)
> . . . Death . . . Friends.

> FARAH
>> (dubious)
>
> It may be so.

KAREN
What is it about then?

FARAH
(beat)
I think it can be about this sound of the roof
when the rains come.

KAREN
That, too.

198/199   EXT. KAREN'S HOUSE—LONG VIEW—DAY

200   Empty. Then Denys's truck moves INTO FRAME. Denys gets
out. Karen comes out of the house. They move slowly toward
each other. No pause as she goes straight into his arms.

201   INT. BEDROOM—KAREN AND DENYS—DAY

Hungry: kissing, holding, touching as they begin undressing
one another.

DENYS'S VOICE
. . . It's the way things are going to be—

201a INT. DINING ROOM—DENYS AND KAREN—NIGHT

GRAMOPHONE MUSIC. She's dressed for dinner.

DENYS
—men who missed moose in Alaska and bear in
America and tigers in India—they're all at sea
now, bound for here.

Karen laughs, then:

KAREN
Berkeley's going to farm— You could do that.

DENYS
No thanks.

104

210 EXT. GRASSY SLOPE—NGONG HILLS—DAY[39]

Their horses graze nearby. They've picnicked. They're quiet, contemplative, lying in the grass.

> KAREN
> There. Where it drops away.
> (then)
> You leave tomorrow . . .

> DENYS
> Yes.

> KAREN
> . . . Doesn't it matter to you that I'm another man's wife?

> DENYS
> (pause)
> What matters to me is that you tried so hard . . . and you're alone now.

> KAREN
> . . . What time tomorrow?

211/212   OMITTED

213   EXT. BERKELEY's house—DAY

Low adobe, quite primitive. Denys's car in front.

214   INT. BERKELEY'S HOUSE—DAY[40]

Dark, Arabic. Berkeley wears a heavy shawl, looks like death. A lovely Somali (MARIAMMO) glides in silently with tea, her eyes anxious for Berkeley.

> BERKELEY
> You don't need *two* guns on safari.

> DENYS
> Do the town work. Outfitting, meeting the clients. There's lots of mail.

201b EXT. THE TERRACE—DENYS—NIGHT

GRAMOPHONE MUSIC CONTINUES. He's in a chair, looking over the lawn. She comes out with the brandy bottle, stops behind him, bends to nuzzle.

> KAREN'S VOICE
> You ought to look in on him. He didn't look that well.

> DENYS'S VOICE
> I have to see him, anyway.

201c INT. KAREN'S BEDROOM—NIGHT

Bamboo-filament light, GRAMOPHONE MUSIC. CLOSE ON their faces, as she makes love to him.

> KAREN'S VOICE
> Can you stay?

> DENYS'S VOICE
> A day or so, is that all right?

> KAREN'S VOICE
> No.

202/205   OMITTED

206   EXT. VERANDA—DENYS AND KAREN—MORNING[35]

They are finishing tea, as Bror's lorry arrives. Denys is still; Karen rises slowly as Bror approches.

> BROR
> (a beat)
> Hello, Denys.

> DENYS
> Blix . . .

> BROR
> (to Karen)
> May I see you, Tanne?

He goes into the house. Karen turns to Denys, hesitates, then moves in after Bror. HOLD ON Denys.

207/208   INT. DRAWING ROOM—KAREN AND BROR—DAY[36]

Bror at the door, Karen near her desk.

> KAREN
> I'm broke, too, you know.

> BROR
> I wouldn't ask, but tips were a bit light.

Resigned, she goes behind her desk to write a check.

> BROR (continuing)
> Are you all right?

> KAREN
> If I get a decent crop.

> BROR
> (grins)
> I could shoot him.

> KAREN
> . . . It won't last.

> BROR
> I've got this horrible urge to kiss you.

She tears out the check, hands it to him.

> BROR (continuing)
> Good luck with it, Tanne. He's smarter than I am: it may go well.

He turns and goes.

208a EXT. VERANDA—DENYS—DAY[37]

As Bror comes out. A beat.

> BROR
> You might have asked, Denys.

106

> DENYS
> I did . . . She said yes.

Karen comes out as Bror moves off. She and Denys are still a moment. Then:

> DENYS (continuing)
> I'm usually glad to see Bror.

> KAREN
> Yes. Everyone likes Bror.
> (beat)
> Don't you want to know what he wanted?

> DENYS
> Yes.

> KAREN
> . . . He wants to come back.

> DENYS
> (pause)
> Don't let him.
> (then)
> I don't think that's what he wanted.

> KAREN
> Damn you, Denys.

209   EXT. THE NGONG HILLS—KAREN AND DENYS—DAY[38]

Riding together up the hill in the wind. The plains s the horizon below.

> KAREN'S VOICE
> I gave him fifty pounds.
> (then)
> If I get eaten up sometime, bury me he you?

> DENYS'S VOICE
> Whatever's left.

107

BERKELEY
Don't know I'd be right for that.

DENYS
You've got to do something.

BERKELEY
I don't actually.
(beat)
My water's gone black, Denys.

Denys looks at him steadily. Drinks.

DENYS
Let's get you to a hospital—get you some proper
care.

BERKELEY
I'm *being* cared for properly.

He glances at Mariammo. Denys follows his gaze, looks back
to Berkeley, who acknowledges with:

BERKELEY (continuing)
It's . . . some years now. She's fond of me, I
think.

DENYS
(stunned)
Why didn't you ever tell me?

BERKELEY
I suppose . . . I think I didn't know you well
enough.

It's as though Denys had been punched. The two friends gaze
at one another a moment.

BERKELEY (continuing)
We've some money left in the trading account.
I'd like my share to go to her.

DENYS
Listen, George Martin had blackwater fever—
when was it? Five years now.

BERKELEY

Mmm.

DENYS

Is there *anything* I can do . . . while you're laid up?

BERKELEY

You might take along that ten-bore you're so fond
of—trigger seems a bit mushy. And the Rigby.
Ask Karen to try it. Nice-size gun for her.

DENYS

Shouldn't you go home for a while?

BERKELEY

Oh . . .
                    (a crooked grin)
I *am* home, I s'pose.

215/216   OMITTED

216a EXT. SCHOOLHOUSE—DAY

The young missionary holds up carved alphabet blocks. The
children CHORUS: e . . . f . . . g . . . etc. CAMERA MOVES TO
Denys, kneeling, juggling pebbles, watching.

Karen, returning from the coffee fields, appears, sees him.

KAREN

Are you packed?

DENYS

Yes.

TRACK WITH them as they walk toward the house.

KAREN

How was town?

DENYS

Crowded.
            (a pause)
I've . . . been thinking. With all the safari work . . .

110

I've got little use for the room . . . at the club.

She looks straight ahead, afraid to speak.

               DENYS (continuing)
I don't know I'd be any good at this, but . . . how
would it be if . . . I kept a few things with you?

She's silent a moment.

               KAREN
You'd come and go from my house . . .

               DENYS
If that's all right.

               KAREN
When the gods want to punish you, they answer
your prayers.

Long silence; then she can contain herself no longer. She
turns, her arms go around him. PUSH TO Denys's face as his
hand presses against the back of her head, hard.

               DENYS
               (quietly)
. . . Berkeley's dying.

She pulls away, searches his face, finds confirmation.

               DENYS (continuing)
He has blackwater fever.

               KAREN
. . . I'll go to him.

               DENYS
No. He . . . wouldn't want you there.

               KAREN
Why?

               DENYS
There's a woman *there*, Karen.

111

(beat)
She's Somali. He's been with her some time now.

                    KAREN
Why didn't you tell me?

                    DENYS
I didn't know. He . . . said he didn't know me well
enough.

He turns, begins walking; she moves after him.

217 EXT. A SMALL CEMETERY—DAY

The grass gone wild. An open grave, thirty to forty settlers,
heads bowed. A minister says the last blessing. Karen looks
toward the fence, where a few Africans watch, among them
Mariammo.

                OLDER KAREN (V.O.)[41]
The friends of the farm came to the house and
went away again. They were not the kind of
people who stay for a long time in the same
place. Neither were they the kind who grow old.
But they had sat contented by the fire, and when
the house, closing round them, said: "I will not
let thee go except thou bless me," they laughed
and blessed it, and it let them go.

As they disperse, Karen passes Mariammo, nods her head
respectfully. Regal, Mariammo looks straight ahead. Lady
Belfield passes Karen.

                LADY BELFIELD
Strange that Denys wasn't here.

                    KAREN
I think . . . he's off with Berkeley.

218 EXT. THE FOREST—DENYS—DAY

Rifle upside-down on his shoulder, stock-still, staring at a
heavy-tusked bull elephant, trunk in the wind, ears spread,
deciding on a charge. A long moment, then Denys FIRES into

112

201b EXT. THE TERRACE—DENYS—NIGHT

GRAMOPHONE MUSIC CONTINUES. He's in a chair, looking over the lawn. She comes out with the brandy bottle, stops behind him, bends to nuzzle.

> KAREN'S VOICE
> You ought to look in on him. He didn't look that well.

> DENYS'S VOICE
> I have to see him, anyway.

201c INT. KAREN'S BEDROOM—NIGHT

Bamboo-filament light, GRAMOPHONE MUSIC. CLOSE ON their faces, as she makes love to him.

> KAREN'S VOICE
> Can you stay?

> DENYS'S VOICE
> A day or so, is that all right?

> KAREN'S VOICE
> No.

202/205 OMITTED

206 EXT. VERANDA—DENYS AND KAREN—MORNING[35]

They are finishing tea, as Bror's lorry arrives. Denys is still; Karen rises slowly as Bror approches.

> BROR
> (a beat)
> Hello, Denys.

> DENYS
> Blix . . .

> BROR
> (to Karen)
> May I see you, Tanne?

He goes into the house. Karen turns to Denys, hesitates, then moves in after Bror. HOLD ON Denys.

207/208   INT. DRAWING ROOM—KAREN AND BROR—DAY[36]

Bror at the door, Karen near her desk.

KAREN

I'm broke, too, you know.

BROR

I wouldn't ask, but tips were a bit light.

Resigned, she goes behind her desk to write a check.

BROR (continuing)

Are you all right?

KAREN

If I get a decent crop.

BROR
(grins)

I could shoot him.

KAREN

. . . It won't last.

BROR

I've got this horrible urge to kiss you.

She tears out the check, hands it to him.

BROR (continuing)

Good luck with it, Tanne. He's smarter than I am: it may go well.

He turns and goes.

208a EXT. VERANDA—DENYS—DAY[37]

As Bror comes out. A beat.

BROR

You might have asked, Denys.

DENYS

I did . . . She said yes.

Karen comes out as Bror moves off. She and Denys are still a
moment. Then:

DENYS (continuing)

I'm usually glad to see Bror.

KAREN

Yes. Everyone likes Bror.
(beat)
Don't you want to know what he wanted?

DENYS

Yes.

KAREN

. . . He wants to come back.

DENYS
(pause)
Don't let him.
(then)
I don't think that's what he wanted.

KAREN

Damn you, Denys.

209   EXT. THE NGONG HILLS—KAREN AND DENYS—DAY[38]

Riding together up the hill in the wind. The plains stretch to
the horizon below.

KAREN'S VOICE

I gave him fifty pounds.
(then)
If I get eaten up sometime, bury me here, will
you?

DENYS'S VOICE

Whatever's left.

210 EXT. GRASSY SLOPE—NGONG HILLS—DAY[39]

Their horses graze nearby. They've picnicked. They're quiet, contemplative, lying in the grass.

> KAREN
> There. Where it drops away.
> (then)
> You leave tomorrow . . .

> DENYS
> Yes.

> KAREN
> . . . Doesn't it matter to you that I'm another man's wife?

> DENYS
> (pause)
> What matters to me is that you tried so hard . . . and you're alone now.

> KAREN
> . . . What time tomorrow?

211/212 OMITTED

213 EXT. BERKELEY'S house—DAY

Low adobe, quite primitive. Denys's car in front.

214 INT. BERKELEY'S HOUSE—DAY[40]

Dark, Arabic. Berkeley wears a heavy shawl, looks like death. A lovely Somali (MARIAMMO) glides in silently with tea, her eyes anxious for Berkeley.

> BERKELEY
> You don't need *two* guns on safari.

> DENYS
> Do the town work. Outfitting, meeting the clients. There's lots of mail.

BERKELEY
Don't know I'd be right for that.

DENYS
You've got to do something.

BERKELEY
I don't actually.
(beat)
My water's gone black, Denys.

Denys looks at him steadily. Drinks.

DENYS
Let's get you to a hospital—get you some proper
care.

BERKELEY
I'm *being* cared for properly.

He glances at Mariammo. Denys follows his gaze, looks back
to Berkeley, who acknowledges with:

BERKELEY (continuing)
It's . . . some years now. She's fond of me, I
think.

DENYS
(stunned)
Why didn't you ever tell me?

BERKELEY
I suppose . . . I think I didn't know you well
enough.

It's as though Denys had been punched. The two friends gaze
at one another a moment.

BERKELEY (continuing)
We've some money left in the trading account.
I'd like my share to go to her.

DENYS
Listen, George Martin had blackwater fever—
when was it? Five years now.

BERKELEY

Mmm.

DENYS

Is there *anything* I can do . . . while you're laid up?

BERKELEY

You might take along that ten-bore you're so fond
of—trigger seems a bit mushy. And the Rigby.
Ask Karen to try it. Nice-size gun for her.

DENYS

Shouldn't you go home for a while?

BERKELEY

Oh . . .
(a crooked grin)
I *am* home, I s'pose.

215/216   OMITTED

216a EXT. SCHOOLHOUSE—DAY

The young missionary holds up carved alphabet blocks. The
children CHORUS: e . . . f . . . g . . . etc. CAMERA MOVES TO
Denys, kneeling, juggling pebbles, watching.

Karen, returning from the coffee fields, appears, sees him.

KAREN

Are you packed?

DENYS

Yes.

TRACK WITH them as they walk toward the house.

KAREN

How was town?

DENYS

Crowded.
(a pause)
I've . . . been thinking. With all the safari work . . .

110

I've got little use for the room . . . at the club.

She looks straight ahead, afraid to speak.

> DENYS (continuing)
> I don't know I'd be any good at this, but . . . how
> would it be if . . . I kept a few things with you?

She's silent a moment.

> KAREN
> You'd come and go from my house . . .

> DENYS
> If that's all right.

> KAREN
> When the gods want to punish you, they answer
> your prayers.

Long silence; then she can contain herself no longer. She
turns, her arms go around him. PUSH TO Denys's face as his
hand presses against the back of her head, hard.

> DENYS
> (quietly)
> . . . Berkeley's dying.

She pulls away, searches his face, finds confirmation.

> DENYS (continuing)
> He has blackwater fever.

> KAREN
> . . . I'll go to him.

> DENYS
> No. He . . . wouldn't want you there.

> KAREN
> Why?

> DENYS
> There's a woman *there*, Karen.

(beat)
She's Somali. He's been with her some time now.

KAREN
Why didn't you tell me?

DENYS
I didn't know. He . . . said he didn't know me well
enough.

He turns, begins walking; she moves after him.

217   EXT. A SMALL CEMETERY—DAY

The grass gone wild. An open grave, thirty to forty settlers,
heads bowed. A minister says the last blessing. Karen looks
toward the fence, where a few Africans watch, among them
Mariammo.

OLDER KAREN (V.O.)[41]
The friends of the farm came to the house and
went away again. They were not the kind of
people who stay for a long time in the same
place. Neither were they the kind who grow old.
But they had sat contented by the fire, and when
the house, closing round them, said: "I will not
let thee go except thou bless me," they laughed
and blessed it, and it let them go.

As they disperse, Karen passes Mariammo, nods her head
respectfully. Regal, Mariammo looks straight ahead. Lady
Belfield passes Karen.

LADY BELFIELD
Strange that Denys wasn't here.

KAREN
I think . . . he's off with Berkeley.

218   EXT. THE FOREST—DENYS—DAY

Rifle upside-down on his shoulder, stock-still, staring at a
heavy-tusked bull elephant, trunk in the wind, ears spread,
deciding on a charge. A long moment, then Denys FIRES into

112

the air. The bull starts, turns, gallops off. Denys turns, starts to walk away, then slowly breaks into a dog trot, his lone figure disappearing among the trees. MUSIC STARTS:

219 A MONTAGE—MUSIC UNDER

A.   KAREN'S GUN RACK. Full with Denys's rifles.

B.   KAREN'S BOOKCASES. Recognize titles from Denys's room at the club.

> OLDER KAREN (V.O.)
> In the days and hours that Denys was at home, we spoke of nothing ordinary, not of my troubles with the farm or of his with his work—

D.   COFFEE FIELDS. Rain.

E.   COFFEE FIELDS. Blossoms.

> OLDER KAREN (V.O.)
> —or of anything at all that was small, and real. We lived disconnected and apart from things.

F.   COFFEE FIELDS. Kikuyu, children and adults pick.

G.   KAREN'S HOUSE. Sunrise. She walks Denys to his lorry, hands him a thermos, kisses him goodbye.

H.   SOAKING VATS. Berries are dumped in.

I.   DRYING TABLES. The beans are mixed and stirred.

> OLDER KAREN (V.O.)
> I had been making up stories while he was away. In the evenings he made himself comfortable, spreading cushions like a couch in front of the fire—

J.   MEDICAL HOUR. Karen, wearing glasses, works on a small child's cut, as the mother holds her.

K.   THE COFFEE SHED. Karen, grave, stares at the pile. Smaller than last year's.

113

OLDER KAREN (V.O.)
—and with me sitting on the floor, cross-legged
like Scheherazade herself, he would listen, clear-
eyed, to a long tale, from when it began until
it ended.

220/221   OMITTED

221a EXT. SHAMBAS—KAREN AND KINANJUI—DAY

Karen is handing Kinanjui a large cake she has made. He
takes it gratefully, when they both hear a DRONING SOUND, and
look up to see a gypsy moth, Denys at the controls, diving low
to buzz her. He points off to where she should meet him. The
natives are stunned speechless. Karen rushes off.

222   EXT. THE MEADOW—DAY

Her car arrives, followed by running natives, as the plane
lands, taxis to her. THEY SHOUT:

KAREN
Where did you get it?

DENYS
Mombasa! Get in!

KAREN
But when did you learn to fly?

DENYS
Yesterday!

She struggles up into the seat in front of him.

223   A FLYING SEQUENCE—DENYS AND KAREN—DAY

A.   Their faces in the wind.

B.   A herd of elephants on the plain.

C.   A soda lake, ringed by flamingoes. At the plane's
approach, thousands of them take off.

114

D.   Karen's hair streaming in the wind.

E.   The Suswa volcano.

F.   A herd of impala streaking across the ground.

G.   The edge of the Rift Valley, higher now. Then beside them, riding the thermals, an eagle.

H.   Denys sees him, is captured. They fly parallel for a moment.

I.   The instrument panel. Silence as Denys cuts the switch.

J.   The smooth rush of air, as eagle and plane glide and turn together. Slowly, they begin to sink.

K.   The eagle. A sharp CRY, and he peels off to soar above them.

L.   Denys. Defeated by gravity. An envious "Damn."

M.   The PROPELLER STARTING.

N.   The trip home. Karen quiet, her cup filled. She reaches back over her shoulder, he reaches forward, and they clasp hands.

224 EXT. THE MEADOW—SUNDOWN

The plane lands. Karen and Denys struggle from their seats. She laughs, tries to speak, can't. He laughs, turns toward the car. She runs after, jumps on his back like a schoolgirl.

DENYS (V.O.)[42]
It's happening so fast . . . Ritchie says it's all shot
out at Maji Moto.

225/253 OMITTED

254 INT. MUTHAIGA CLUB—NIGHT[43]

Monte Carlo night: wheel of chance, dice, chemin

115

de fer. Some new faces. Denys has been talking to Delamere and ANOTHER MAN. (Continuation from above.)

DELAMERE

You talk as if it's Sussex . . . we haven't even touched this continent yet.

DENYS

No, D.—we're getting too good at it: smokeless powder, magnum loads. Better rifles every year . . . Too damn many people doing it.

255   ANOTHER AREA—KAREN AND FELICITY[44]

Felicity plays the wheel of chance, as Karen stands with her in mid-conversation. A YOUNG MAN is there.

FELICITY

You think he'd take me up sometime?

KAREN

(no pause)
I don't know. How's your new pony?

FELICITY

Green. But willing. I thought I'd show him at Nanyuki.

YOUNG MAN

Care to wager, Baroness?

KAREN

No, thank you.

255a DENYS AND GERMAN COUPLE[45]

Delamere has left. Denys is trying to get away from the clients.

WIFE

But you'll have time for lunch, won't you, before we leave?

DENYS

I'd like to, but I'm going right back out. The

116

taxidermist's just across from the station. You can't miss it.

The man has taken out some bills, offers them to DENYS.

> MAN
> Wonderful trip, Denys, wonderful.

> DENYS
> (holds up hand)
> Not necessary . . . thank you.

The man stuffs the bills into Denys's pocket.

> MAN
> Don't be silly. Wonderful trip!

CAMERA FINDS KAREN, who sees the exchange. FOLLOW HER GAZE back to Denys and the couple.

> WIFE
> You come to see us if you get to Munich!

> DENYS
> . . . Absolutely.

255b KAREN AND FELICITY[46]

Karen still gazing toward Denys.

> YOUNG MAN
> Did you hear? . . . Belfield's stepping down.

Delamere moves past. Felicity stops him with:

> FELICITY
> D.? What was the commotion in the bar when we came in?

> DELAMERE
> The Americans are teaching us about poker. Blix is down a few hundred, but we're otherwise all right.

Karen's head whirls around toward Delamere.

255c INT. MEN'S BAR—MUTHAIGA CLUB—NIGHT[47]

Not crowded. Bror, at poker table, his back to door. The Huge Man plays chess. Shock as Karen enters.

> BROR
> (turning)
> What is it, Tanne?

> KAREN
> May I see you, please?

He goes to her, moves her toward the door. She'll resist. They keep their voices low.

> BROR
> You don't belong in here, you know that.

> KAREN
> What are you doing—?

> HUGE MAN
> Von Bixen! Get that woman out of here!

BROR propels her. She pulls away.

> KAREN
> You *owe* me that money!

> BROR
> You'll be all right; ask your lover.

She slaps him hard. He flushes. The room is embarrassed. A beat between them. She leaves.

255d INT. MUTHAIGA CLUB—PARTY[48]

Karen returns, looks off. CAMERA follows her gaze to see Denys dancing with a radiant Felicity. INTERCUT Karen watching them.

255e EXT. THE ROAD—DENYS'S CAR—NIGHT[49]

Karen and Denys ride in silence a moment.

KAREN

You can't hunt forever. Why don't you help me with the farm? It looks to be a good crop this year. We could go partners.

DENYS

And when we voted opposite . . .

KAREN

I'd give in.

DENYS

I wouldn't like that.

KAREN

Someone has to.

DENYS

No. I don't believe that.
(then)
You don't see the farms from where I do, Karen: from the air. They're taking Africa.
(then)
I don't like farms.

KAREN

They'll all go wild again, you said.

DENYS

. . . I may have been wrong.

255f EXT. VERANDA—KAREN AND DENYS—MORNING (RAIN)[50]

Tea and rolls on a small table. Denys sips tea, abruptly gets up, paces, stops to search the sky. Karen watches, opens a book. He turns, sees her look, moves to her, bends to kiss her hair, goes into the house. She is not reassured.

255g INT. BANKER'S OFFICE—KAREN AND BANKER—DAY

A number of polo trophies. The BANKER has a stump where his left hand should be. As he writes:

BANKER

How many acres under cultivation?

119

                    KAREN
Five hundred.

                    BANKER
The rest of it's wild?

                    KAREN
My Kikuyu live there.

                    BANKER
Why don't you move them off?

                    KAREN
Because they *live* there.

                    BANKER
Not much use to make of it.
                    (then)
We'll take it over should you default.

255h EXT. BANK—NAIROBI—FARAH—DAY

Waiting as she approaches.

                    KAREN
We've got another year.

                    FARAH
God is great, msabu.

                    KAREN
He's charging three percent.

255i EXT. THE FARM—KAREN, FARAH, NATIVES, YOUNG MAN—DAY[51]

Several natives strain to hold up a wagon from which one
wheel's removed. Karen, hands filthy, greases the axle. An
earnest YOUNG MAN in corduroy, map spread out before him,
is in mid-sales pitch.

                    KAREN
There's a road there already.

                    YOUNG MAN
It's a track, really—this will be a proper road—

gravel, a lane each way. Then, if you'll stand the extra cost, we'll bring it on out to you.

How much would it be?

(rolling map)
Say . . . two hundred pounds.

Good Lord.

That's just *our* cost, actually; we thought you'd want it.

That's kind of you—I suppose I like the old road, really. Can I get you tea?

Mustn't, thanks: I've got my Kukes working down the way. Leave them alone—you know how they are.

(not unkindly)
No. I've never really known how they are at all.

Cheery-bye, then.

He leaves. Farah, fastidious, looks at Karen's hands.

These Kikuyu can do this work.

Yes. They're not afraid to get dirty. Like the Somali.

Farah frowns. The Kikuyu think this is very funny.

121

FARAH
I think Bedar can come today.

KAREN
Bedar is in the Mara.

FARAH
It may be so, msabu. Unless he comes today.

255j OMITTED

255k EXT. THE FARM—KAREN—DAY[52]

Late afternoon. Tired, she walk home alone. Faint, O.S.,
MOZART. She walks quickly, breaks into a run.

255l EXT. THE TERRACE—DENYS—DAY[53]

Dirty, exhausted, fast asleep in the lounge chair, his glass in
his lap. The light fading.

The gramophone outside, the record finishes, keeps revolving.

Karen ENTERS SHOT, slows. Quiet, she'll take the needle from
the record, get her straight chair and place it—just so—next
to his, take the glass from his lap, sit. And touch his chair.

255m WIDE VIEW ACROSS THE LAWN—KAREN—KAREN AND DENYS—
DUSK[54]

A portrait. Of them, and another era, soon to end.

KAREN (V.O.)
How could Farah know just when you'd come.

DENYS (V.O.)
. . . Africa.

255n EXT. MEADOW—DENYS'S PLANE—SUNRISE[55]

From a distance, Karen waves as the plane takes off.

DENYS (V.O.)
I may be a little longer this time. I've got to go
farther to find a good camp.

CAMERA PUSHES TO KAREN, as she watches the plane.

> KAREN
> (quietly, to herself)
> . . . Goodbye again.

256   OMITTED

257   INT. KITCHEN—KAREN AND KAMANTE—DAY[56]

He is dicing vegetables; she's arranging flowers.

> KAMANTE
> When you go in the sky with Bedar, do you see
> God?

> KAREN
> No.

> KAMANTE
> Ahh. Then you do not go up high enough.
> (he chops)
> Do you think sometime you will go up high
> enough to see him?

> KAREN
> No. I don't know.

> KAMANTE
> Then I do not know at all why you go to fly.

Farah enters.

> FARAH
> Msabu, Chief Kinanjui has come to see you.

258   EXT. TERRACE—FARAH, KINANJUI AND KAREN—DAY[57]

Many natives watch from a respectful distance as Kinanjui,
frail, leaning on a stick, finishes addressing Karen in Swahili.
A grave pause. Then:

> FARAH
> This chief says . . . tall children can come to

123

school now, msabu.

FEATURE Karen's strong reaction. A moment. Then:

> KAREN
> Tell Chief Kinanjui that reading is a valuable
> thing. His children will remember him well.

Farah translates. Kinanjui pauses thoughtfully, then speaks in
Swahili, turns with dignity, moves off.

> FARAH
> This chief says . . . people who read do also
> foolish things.

Over Kinanjui's departing figure:

LONG DISSOLVE TO:

258a EXT. THE LAWN—CHRISTMAS TREE—NIGHT[58]

Small candles burn on every branch. PULL BACK: Karen receives
a line of natives, who greet her, then move to the table where
Farah doles out tobacco, sugar, candy. A bonfire. Study the
African faces.

A MAN of fifty, gnarled, his dignity untarnished. A TOOTHLESS
CRONE, grinning. A YOUNG MOTHER, sleek and shy. A BOY OF
TEN who has claimed a place in line.

Over this, VOCAL MUSIC, a cappella, in Swahili.

258b EXT. POLO FIELD—NAIROBI—DAY

Hell-for-leather, no uniforms or helmets, settlers versus Gov-
ernment House. Cars, carriages, spectators line the field. Much
drinking, shouting. The referee FIRES A PISTOL when the ball
goes out of bounds. Bror's a contestant, but the action belongs
to Felicity, now twenty-one, expert, reckless, striking, one of
two women on the field.

She and a male opponent are after the ball, racing stride for
stride for half the field, ponies bumping, elbows flying. She
rides him off the ball and with a looping backhand, drives it
home. The referee FIRES.

LADY BELFIELD

Quite something, Felicity.

KAREN

Yes, indeed.

Bror slides off his horse near them, laughing, gives up his place to a replacement, takes champagne. Lady Delamere turns away as Bror comes to Karen.

BROR

How are you, Tanne?

KAREN

Getting old, I think: not you. How's the hunting?

BROR

I'll make a living.
(beat)
Where's Denys?

KAREN

Uganda. Some potentate.

BROR
(sips)
I thought you might be wanting a divorce.

KAREN
(beat)
Has she got money?
(at his grin)
Of course she's got money.
(beat)
Is this important, Bror?

BROR
(shrugs)
I suppose.

KAREN

. . . I'll have to accuse you of something, you know.
(then)

125

Or did you think you'd have it the other way
round?

> BROR
>
> No, fire away. Whatever, I've surely done it.
> (serious)
> Thank you, Tanne.

A moment:

> KAREN
> How do you manage it . . . to keep us friends?

> BROR
> We started that way.

> KAREN
> (nods, then)
> I'll be happy for you. If I can.

He kisses her lightly. A half smile.

> BROR
> I remember that. Quite well.

He offers a small salute, turns away, at once caught up in the
crowd. Karen finds a cigarette. Her hands are shaking. A
chapter ends.

258c EXT. THE AFRICAN COASTLINE—AERIAL—DAY

RUSHING low above dazzling beach and rolling surf. ANGLE
ADJUSTS to include the shadow of an airplane.

> DENYS (V.O.)
> How was the crop?

> KAREN (V.O.)
> Disappointing . . . What I need is a swim in
> somebody's ocean.

258d EXT. THE BEACH—WIDE ANGLE—DAY

Perhaps the plane visible on the beach. Denys makes a fire;

126

Karen brings supplies from the plane.

                    DENYS (V.O.)
     I can fix *that*, I think.

258e EXT. THE BEACH—KAREN AND DENYS—NIGHT[59]

     A small fire. Wine, the remains of shellfish. She's in a caftan;
     he toys with the fire. They are quiet.

                    KAREN
     When you go away, on safari . . . are you ever
     with someone else?

                    DENYS
                   (surprised)
     I'd be with you if I wanted to be with anyone.

                    KAREN
     . . . Do you feel lonely?

                    DENYS
     Sometimes.

                    KAREN
     Do you ever wonder if I might be lonely?

                    DENYS
     . . . No. I don't.

                    KAREN
     Do you think about me at all?

                    DENYS
     Yes. Often.

                    KAREN
     But not enough to come back.

                    DENYS
     I do come back.

A beat of silence. He pokes at the fire again.

KAREN

Bror's asked for a divorce. He's found someone
he wants to marry.
(silence)
I thought *we* might do that someday.

DENYS

Divorce?
(beat)
How would a wedding change things?

KAREN

I might like it.
(then)
What's wrong with marriage?

DENYS

I don't know that I'd do it well.
(pause)
Have you ever seen one you admired?

KAREN
(admits)
No.
(then)
Well . . . The Belfields.

DENYS

He sent her home for the rains in 1910 and
didn't tell her they were over until 1913.

KAREN

I *would* like someone to ask sometime. Do that,
will you? If I promise to say no?

DENYS
(grins)
Just trust you, eh?

Silence. Then.

KAREN

When you go away . . . you don't always go on
safari . . . do you.

128

                    DENYS
                  (long beat)
    . . . No.

                    KAREN
You just want to be away.

                    DENYS
Sometimes . . . I do.
                  (pause)
It's not meant to hurt you.

                    KAREN
It does.

                    DENYS
    I know.

258f EXT. VERY HIGH AERIAL—DAY

    Looking down on the biplane, very small, lonely in the dawn
    sky, flying above a great sweep of Africa.

258g INT. DRAWING ROOM—KAREN AND BELKNAP—NIGHT[60]

    Belknap, in wet slicker, stands before the table where her
    books lie. She licks an envelope. O.S. RAIN.

                    KAREN
    It hasn't been your fault, I just can't afford to
    keep you.

                    BELKNAP
    I figured. I had enough of Africa, anyway.

                    KAREN
                  (gives him envelope)
    Your wages. There's a bonus there, not much of
    one. If you'll stop at Muthaiga Club, they've a
    ticket for you. As far as New York: I didn't know
    how to do Ohio.

                    BELKNAP
. . . That's too much, Miz Blixen.

                    129

                              KAREN
Not for home.

                             BELKNAP
Always earned my way. Till now.
                          (turns to go)
You're wrong about keeping this place, but I
hope you make it.

                              KAREN
Safe home, Mister Belknap.

258h EXT. POND—DAY—(RAIN)

A rush of water pours through a fault in the dam. ANGLE
WIDENS to see Karen, thigh deep in water, packing bags of dirt
into the breach. Natives work nearby, supervised by Farah,
but they see how hopeless it is. At last Karen straightens.
Quietly:

                              KAREN
Let it go . . .
                        (wryly, to Farah)
This water lives in Mombasa, anyway.

258i EXT. DOWNTOWN SQUARE—STATUE—DAY[61]

A large bronze statue is unveiled. A small BAND PLAYS. Natives
gape at it. Karen and Farah stare from her car. FEATURE her
reaction.

258j EXT. THE SKY—DENYS'S PLANE—DAY

He looks out over the side to see:

1. RAILROAD TRACKS. Sun glinting off them, land being cleared
    ahead.

Wider view of Denys in the plane. He looks off;

2. TELEPHONE POLES. Running along the road.

Tighter view of Denys in the plane.

3. REFUSE. Jam tins, and paper sacks left by hunting parties
    in the meadows.

                              130

259 OMITTED

260 INT. DRAWING ROOM—KAREN AND DENYS—NIGHT

He sits leaning over a map spread on the floor. She's in a chair with clothes to mend.

> DENYS
> I flew as far as Narok: you can see the ruts where the lorries have been. The Serengeti's still good
> . . .

> KAREN
> It would take a week just getting there.

> DENYS
> More like ten days . . . Samburu still seems good.
> (then)
> I haven't seen Belknap.

> KAREN
> He must be in America by now.
> (at his look)
> I let him go . . . I had to.
> (then)
> But you don't really want to know about the farm, do you.

He's silent. She finishes mending her trousers, picks up his shirt.

> KAREN (continuing)
> Have you got buttons anywhere?

> DENYS
> What are you doing?

> KAREN
> Mending your shirt.

> DENYS
> I have that done in town.

She stares. He returns to the map. A beat.

DENYS (continuing)
I'll try Samburu. Day after tomorrow.

KAREN
(quietly)
You just got back.

DENYS
(a beat)
Felicity's asked to come along. I started to say no
. . . because I thought *you* wouldn't like it.
(silence)
There's no reason for her not to come.

KAREN
Yes there is. I *wouldn't* like it.
(silence)
Do you want her along?

DENYS
I want things that don't matter not to matter.

KAREN
Then tell her no. Do it for me.

DENYS
And then? What else will there be?

KAREN
Why is your freedom more important than mine?

DENYS
I've *never* interfered with you.

KAREN
I'm not allowed to need you. Rely on you. Expect
anything at all. I'm only free to leave.
(then)
But I *do* need you.

DENYS
There's no answer to that, Karen. Suppose I
died? Would you die? You don't *need* me. You
mix up need with want. You always have.

132

KAREN

My God. In the world you'd make, there'd be no
love at all.

DENYS

Or the best kind. The kind we wouldn't have to
prove.

KAREN

You'll live on the moon, then—

DENYS

—Why? Because I won't do it your way? Are
we assuming there's one *proper* way to do all
this?
(*beat*)
Do you think I care about Felicity?

KAREN

No.

DENYS

Do you think I'll be involved with her?

KAREN

No.

DENYS

Then there's no reason for this, is there?

KAREN

I want you to give it up. For me.

He holds her gaze.

KAREN (continuing)

I've learned a thing you haven't. There *are* things
worth having—they come at a price. I want to
be one of them.
(beat)
I won't allow it, Denys.

DENYS
(beat)

You've no idea, have you—the effect that language has.

> KAREN
> I used to think there was nothing you really wanted. But that's not it, is it? You want it all.

> DENYS
> I want it . . . a better way.
> (then)
> I'm going to Samburu. She can come or not.

> KAREN
> Then you'll be living elsewhere.

> DENYS
> . . . All right.

She gets up. As she goes:

> KAREN[62]
> I didn't want your soul, Denys—I was only trying to mend your shirt.

261 EXT. COFFEE FIELDS—A TREE—DAY

Heavy with clumps of red berries. INTO FRAME: Black hands, nimble and quick, stripping the ripe coffee.

262 EXT. COFFEE SHED—DAY

A long wooden water trough, thick with bobbing berries: black hands—one pair of white discard green ones.

263 INT. THE SHED—DAY

Berries in the soaking tank. The Kikuyu jovial: this crop's a good one. KAREN sips tea, cheerless.

264 EXT. DRYING TABLES—KAREN AND NATIVES—DAY

She's in different clothes, spreading the husked coffee to dry in the sun. The Kikuyu know she's upset, know to leave her alone.

265 INT. THE SHED—NIGHT

Kerosene lamps, CLANKING MACHINERY: A HUGE REVOLVING DRUM, heated by a wood-burning furnace stoked by sweating Kikuyu. Karen watches dispassionately.

266 INT. KAREN'S BEDROOM—NIGHT

She's at her vanity, combing her hair, hollow-eyed. The owl watches her. She taps its beak.

                              KAREN
              Is that a prince in there?

267 INT. KAREN'S BEDROOM—LANTERN—NIGHT

The flame FILLING FRAME. It is carried over to her bed and reveals Kamante, holding it, shaking her. As she comes awake with a start:

                            KAMANTE
              I think that you had better get up, memsaab.

                              KAREN
              What . . . ?

                            KAMANTE
              I think that you had better get up, memsaab, I
              think that God is coming.

She struggles out of bed. Sees something out the window, moves to it. The skyline is an eerie orange. Now the SOUND OF SHOUTING, RUNNING. She runs out.

268 EXT. COFFEE SHED—NIGHT

Hundreds of Kikuyu silent in the glow of a huge fire, some with useless buckets. The entire structure is ablaze, the crop inside destroyed.

Karen watches, detached, a spectator. A toddler comes to her, hands at the pocket of her robe where there might be candy. When she kneels to the child—strangely—it has her full attention. She pokes the child, tickles it.

KAREN

All gone.

She watches the fire, hand idle on the child.

269 EXT. COFFEE SHED—WIDE ANGLE—DAY

Still smoldering. Kikuyu children dash hotfooted in the charred remains, salvaging things. Karen, dirty, stands with **Delamere**, surveying it. Farah is in b.g. She's nearly gay, brittle, **as they** walk.

DELAMERE

Insurance?

KAREN

That's for pessimists.

DELAMERE

What about your family?

KAREN

They write. To say I've squandered their money.

DELAMERE

. . . Where is Denys?

KAREN
(laughs, too bright)

Who knows?
(beat)
Doesn't matter. The baroness is broke, D. It's over.
(beat)
I've got to get a bit of land before I go . . . for my Kikuyu.

DELAMERE

You've trouble enough, Karen—don't get into that.

KAREN

Just a chunk somewhere—enough that they can all stay together.

136

They've reached Farah.

> FARAH
> I can go now, for Bedar.

> KAREN
> No.
> (to Delamere)
> We're fresh out of coffee—but I can give you
> tea.

270 INT. COMMISSIONER'S OFFICE—KAREN—DAY

She has tea. He's in uniform.

> COMMISSIONER
> There's no arable land that size outside the re-
> serve—if there were, we'd not put natives on it.

> KAREN
> Since it's theirs—

> COMMISSIONER
> —It belongs to the Crown, Baroness. What you
> want is quite impossible.

> KAREN
> Yes, it always is. Who must I see next?

270a INT. SECOND COMMISSIONER'S OFFICE—DAY

As though a direct continuation.

> SECOND COMMISSIONER
> You've run through us all, I'm afraid.

She stands, puts on her gloves.

> KAREN
> We've a new governor, haven't we?

> SECOND COMMISSIONER
> Sir Joseph? He's not arrived yet.

137

KAREN

But will soon, I'm told.
(smiles)
You *do* still ask me to things?

270b EXT. KAREN'S HOUSE—DAY[63]

Karen, formally dressed, comes out with Farah. As they start
toward the car, she stops. CAMERA REVEALS twenty or thirty
Kikuyu from the shambas, grouped around the front lawn,
staring quietly at her. Some women have bundles of sticks on
their bent backs. No one speaks. Karen looks back at them.
Then moves slowly to her car, Farah following.

271/272   OMITTED

273   EXT. GOVERNOR'S RESIDENCE—WIDE—DAY

An afternoon reception on the lawn. A long reception line,
after which there are buffet tables, bar. A canopy covers the
tables.

MOVE CLOSER to the reception line. The First Commissioner is
performing introductions. Karen waits.

COMMISSIONER

The Honorable Hugh Chomondeley, Lord Delamere.

SIR JOSEPH

Delamere.

DELAMERE

Your servant, sir.

KAREN

Commissioner.

COMMISSIONER

Baroness.

As the Commissioner turns to present her, CAMERA SEES a
lorry arriving in b.g. Denys gets out. He's in safari clothes,

138

dusty, sweaty. He walks across toward the reception line, his dress drawing a few disapproving glances. CAMERA TAKES US to Karen.

> SIR JOSEPH
> I'm sorry to know that Kenya will be losing you.

> KAREN
> You've heard of my trouble.

> SIR JOSEPH
> Yes. I regret it.

> KAREN
> Do you know of my problem now?

> SIR JOSEPH
> This land you want from us.

> KAREN
> Will you help me, Sir Joseph?

> COMMISSIONER
> Baroness, this really isn't—

> SIR JOSEPH
> —That's quite difficult.

The line begins to BUZZ. Denys arrives now, just as Karen suddenly kneels before Sir Joseph, takes time to arrange her skirt. A gasp. Denys is riveted.

> SIR JOSEPH (continuing)
> Please get up, Baroness.

> KAREN
> Kenya is a hard country for women, so there's a chivalry here, of a sort. You're a powerful man. And I've no one else to turn to.

> SIR JOSEPH
> Please—let's discuss this in a proper way, can't we?

139

KAREN

You mustn't be embarrassed. I've lost everything—it costs me very little to beg you.

The Commissioner has motioned for an officious AIDE. Sir
Joseph's wife, LADY BYRNE, regal, watches Karen. Denys is
grave, taking this in.

KAREN (continuing)

The land was theirs, you see: we took it. And
now they've nowhere to go.

The Aide arrives, would lift her to her feet, but:

DENYS

No . . . Give her a moment, please.

Karen turns, is stunned. Her gaze holds his.

SIR JOSEPH

I'll look into it. We'll do the best we can.

She pulls her eyes from Denys.

KAREN

May I have your word?

LADY BYRNE

You have mine, madam.

Karen rises, brushes her skirt, nods thanks to Sir Joseph,
offers her hand to Lady Byrne.

KAREN

I hope you'll be happy here. I was.

LADY BYRNE

I'm sorry I won't know you.

Karen curtsies, turns away. CAMERA FOLLOWS as Denys falls in
beside her, walking across the lawn toward her car. A few
guests glance and whisper as they pass. A beat:

140

DENYS

. . . I didn't hear till I'd got to the border.

KAREN

It seems I'll do most anything to get your attention.
(then)
I've almost got you packed. Your books and . . . I
wonder what will happen now.
(a beat)
I've got to think what I'll do. Sometimes I wonder
if I could write. Not well but to make a living.
D'you think?

DENYS

I don't know.

KAREN

My poor family. I've got them near bankrupt;
now I'll have to ask for more help.

They arrive at her car, where Farah waits respectfully. Perhaps
he bows to Denys.

DENYS

. . . I've got some money, Karen.

KAREN

. . . You'd keep me then.
(silence)
Too late . . . I've got the bug. I want to be worth
something.

DENYS

. . . What *will* you do?

KAREN

After my rummage sale . . . Leave. Friday. For
Mombasa. And the boat to Denmark.

Denys weighs this. In the silence, Karen looks back at the
reception, then to Denys.

KAREN (continuing)

Thank you, Denys.

She gets in the car, Farah following, and drives away. CAMERA HOLDS on Denys.

273a EXT. THE FARM—KIKUYU—DAY

They stand silently, staring toward the house. PAN SLOWLY TOWARD THE HOUSE.

274 INT. LIVING ROOM—KAREN AND FARAH—DAY

She's moving through, tagging pieces of furniture. As she does, the Kikuyu move the pieces outside. Farah follows her. She works as she talks.

KAREN
You must have them ready to leave before the rains. It is good land, enough for all, and they must not fight about it or be any trouble to the authorities—do you understand—or they will lose it.

FARAH
Yes, msabu.

KAREN
You must make them understand that I will not be here to speak for them.

FARAH
This land is far?

KAREN
By Dagoretti. Not too far.

FARAH
Msabu? How can it be now, with me and yourself?

KAREN
You will have some money. Enough, I think.

FARAH
I do not speak of money.

142

KAREN
(beat)
Do you remember how it was on safari? In the
afternoons, I would send you ahead, to find a
place and wait for me?

FARAH
And you can see the fire and come to this place.

KAREN
Yes. Well, it is like that. Only this time, I am
going first, to wait for you.

FARAH
(considers, then)
It is far where you are going?

KAREN
Yes.

FARAH
You must make this fire very big. So I can find
you.

Her back to him. She points to the andirons:

KAREN
Take those on to the lawn.

Because she's crying. Alone she breaks down.

275   INT. DINING ROOM—CLOSE—GRAMOPHONE—NIGHT

Playing a waltz. WIDEN TO REVEAL the dining room nearly bare,
as it was when she first came. She has dined alone, the can-
delabra gone, a stubbly candle lighting the table.

The SOUND OF A TRUCK outside. She recognizes it. Waits. After
a beat, Denys comes in. A pause.

KAREN
Have you had dinner?

He nods, but moves to sit. Juma brings a glass, pours some
wine for him.

143

KAREN (continuing)
I was going to send your things to the club, is
that all right?

As Juma starts to go:

KAREN (continuing)
Juma?

He moves to her. She reaches out, takes off his gloves.

KAREN (continuing)
This wasn't a very good idea.

Juma grins, goes off. Karen looks at the empty room.

KAREN (continuing)
We should have had it this way all the time.

DENYS
I don't know. I was beginning to like your things.

KAREN
. . . and I was beginning to like being without
them.

Beat between them. Then:

DENYS
You've ruined it for me, you know.

KAREN
Ruined . . . ?

DENYS
Solitude . . . Being alone.

KAREN
(quietly)
. . . Have I?

DENYS
Let me . . . I'd like to fly you to Mombasa.

144

KAREN

. . . All right. When?

DENYS

I've got something to arrange tomorrow. Near
Tsavo. But I'll be back early enough on Friday.
Will that be all right?

KAREN

Of course.

DENYS

Promise you'll wait.

KAREN

I promise.
(then)
I've got this little thing I've learned to do just
lately . . . When it's so hard I think I shan't go
on, I try to make it worse. I make myself think
about Berkeley. Our camp on the river. How
good it was. When I'm certain I won't stand it, I
go a moment more. Then I know I can bear
anything.

She stubs out her cigarette, then smiles.

KAREN (continuing)

Would you like to help me?

DENYS

Yes.

KAREN (holds out hand)

Come dance with me then.

He rises, goes to her, takes her in his arms, waltzes her through
and out to:

276/277   EXT. THE TERRACE—KAREN AND DENYS—NIGHT

In a spill of light from the dining room, he slowly dances her
across the terrace. She kicks off her shoes as they move out into
the moonlight. The lawn is strewn with her tagged furniture.

145

KAREN'S VOICE

You were right, you know. The farm never was
mine . . . It belongs to Africa.

DENYS'S VOICE[64]

Or God . . . if He wants it.

OLDER KAREN (V.O.)

I had a farm in Africa . . .

DENYS'S VOICE

But . . . I may have been wrong.

PULL AWAY until we almost lose them in the dark. SOUND OF
SINGING in Swahili on soundtrack.

278   EXT. THE LAWN—HIGH ANGLE—DAY

From the same position. Now the lawn is filled with shoppers.
Working-class people, no one we have seen before. They paw
over her things. SOUND OF SINGING PERSISTS.

279/281   OMITTED

282   EXT. AFRICA—WIDE VISTA—DAY

Vast. Unending. Empty. HOLD. HOLD. SINGING FADES.

LONG DISSOLVE TO:

283   EXT. THE LAWN—DAY

The last of the sale, most items gone. Karen, in different
clothes, looks to the terrace.

Farah, hands behind his back, is searching the sky; he looks to
Karen, then back to the sky.

Karen is frightened. She turns, goes into the house.

284   EXT. THE HOUSE—BROR—SUNSET

He arrives in his car, goes slowly into the house.

146

She's on the floor, with the last of her crates. He enters. She looks at him. A long moment. She picks up a book, leafs through it. He waits. In time:

> KAREN
> Hello, Bror.
> (beat)
> Do you want a drink?

> BROR
> Please.

But she doesn't move. Finally:

> KAREN
> I haven't got one.

He moves to her. He kneels, takes the book from her.

> BROR
> (very gently)
> Tanne? Denys has been killed. His plane crashed at Tsavo.

> KAREN
> Was he damaged?

She might as well have struck him. He stands.

> BROR
> There was a fire.
> (beat)
> I'll take you into town.

> KAREN
> (quietly)
> Why did they send you?

> BROR
> I . . . thought I should.

147

KAREN
(beat)
My God, you're brave.

286 EXT. NGONG HILLS—WHITE SCREEN—DAY

Mist. It's clearing. As it does, we see the gravesite Karen
selected for herself. In f.g. three Kikuyu, who've dug the
grave, move away. In b.g. a procession of cars and lorries stops.
So far away we can't make them out, people debark; men take
the coffin from a truck.

287 VERY WIDE ANGLE—THE PROCESSION—DAY

Delamere, others, as pallbearers. The MINISTER, thirty and
some mourners. Bror with his new wife. And Karen, just
behind the coffin.

288 EXT. THE GRAVE—FUNERAL—DAY

The coffin in the ground. Karen nearest the grave. At a
distance, a few Africans.

MINISTER
—The sun shall not smite thee by day, nor the
moon at night. The Lord shall preserve thee
from all evil; He shall preserve thy soul.

Karen turns suddenly to look up the hill. FOLLOW
her gaze to see a lone Masai with a spear at the
crest. PAN BACK to the grave during:

MINISTER (continuing)
The Lord shall preserve thy going out and thy
coming in, from this time forth and even for-
evermore.

ALL
Amen.

The Minister steps back, looks to Karen, who still stares up
the hill. She runs her fingers through her hair. She's gaunt,
beautiful. She opens one of Denys's books. Her voice is low,
steady, clear.

"The time you won your town the race
We chaired you through the marketplace;
Man and boy stood cheering by
And home we brought you, shoulder-high."

PAN THE mourners. Men swallow. Some women begin to cry.
Bror is stoic, Felicity brave.

KAREN'S VOICE (continuing)
"Smart lad, to slip betimes away
From fields where glory does not stay,
And early though the laurel grows
It withers quicker than a rose."

PAN TO Karen.

KAREN (continuing)
"Now you will not swell the rout
Of lads that wore their honors out
Runners whom renown outran
And the name died 'fore the man."

Not a tear. She no longer needs the book.

KAREN (continuing)
"And round that early-laureled head
Will flock to gaze the strengthless dead
And find unwithered on its curls
A garland . . . briefer than a girl's."

Pause. She looks back up the hill. FOLLOW HER LOOK: the crest
is bare. COME BACK TO Karen, voice unsteady.

KAREN (continuing)
Now take back the soul of Denys George Finch-
Hatton, whom You have shared with us. He
brought us joy . . . we loved him well.
                    (kneels, then)
He was not ours.
                    (long beat)
He was not mine.

149

She takes a handful of earth to drop into the grave. Her lips move: perhaps "I love we"—we don't hear. But she cannot drop the earth; the gesture is too final. Some trickles away through her hand. Still clutching what is left, she walks away, not toward the cars, but down the face of the hill, where Farah waits. She stops once to take off her shoes.

289 EXT. THE FARM—KAREN—DAY

Saying goodbye. Dressed for travel she walks:

A. The coffee fields.

B. The shambas. Elders are quiet, watchful, the small children follow her silently. Perhaps she passes the cuckoo clock, hanging on Kinanjui's old hut.

C. The schoolhouse.

D. The front of the house, where she fondly touches both Juma and Kamante. DURING ABOVE WE HEAR:

> OLDER KAREN (V.O.)[65]
> If I know a song of Africa, of the giraffe and the African new moon lying on her back, of the plows in the fields and the sweaty faces of the coffee pickers, does Africa know a song of me? Will the air over the plain quiver with a color that I have had on, or the children invent a game in which my name is, or the full moon throw a shadow over the gravel of the drive that was like me, or will the eagles of the Ngong Hills look out for me?

290 OMITTED

291 INT. MUTHAIGA CLUB—LOBBY—KAREN—DAY

At the desk, writing out last instructions.

> KAREN
> —letters just send on to this address in Denmark. My accounts should go to Bunter and

Company—and anything else you don't know
what to do with.

Yes, memsaab.

As she turns, the Young Man who tried to sell her the new
road approaches.

KAREN

I still like the old road better.

YOUNG MAN
(grins)
Yes, Baroness. I've been sent to ask if we might
stand you a drink.

KAREN

And who is we?

YOUNG MAN

Well . . . the members, actually.

She nods, walks with him to the Men's Bar entrance.

292   INT. MEN'S BAR—DAY

Thirty men, many we know, and the Huge Man. A few standing; most sit. They don't acknowledge her. She goes straight
to the bar.

KAREN

Whiskey, please.

The native barman hesitates, looks to the Young Man.

YOUNG MAN

Two whiskeys, please.

Behind her, the SCRAPING OF CHAIRS.

YOUNG MAN
(continuing, raising glass)
The king, I guess.

KAREN
(beat)
Rose-lipt maidens. Lightfoot lads.

Behind her, all the men are standing. Some conversation continues, only a few look at her, but they are damn well on their feet, including the Huge Man. She knocks back her drink.

KAREN (continuing)
Thank you.

And walks briskly through the door.

292a INT. STATION—CLOUD OF STEAM NEAR TRAIN—DAY

It clears to reveal Farah and Karen, holding Dusk's leash, standing in front of the train. She fondles him, then hands the leash to Farah.

KAREN[66]
He is old now. Like you and me. He should die where he lived. Will you keep him for me, till then?

FARAH
Yes, msabu.

He snaps his fingers. The dog sits. TRAIN WHISTLE. Karen takes her compass from her purse.

KAREN
This is dear to me: it has helped me find my way. I leave it with you to help you search for me.

He takes it. She turns away, stops. A moment. Then, without turning back or looking at him:

KAREN
(continuing, quietly)
I want to hear you say my name.

152

FARAH

. . . You are Karen, msabu.

KAREN[67]

Goodbye, Farah Aden.

FARAH

I will find you, msabu.

As she moves away, STEAM AGAIN FILLS THE FRAME.

293   EXT. NGONG HILLS—WIDE VIEW—DAY

Above the grave, Africa spread out below. A black-maned lion
walks slowly through the grass.

OLDER KAREN (V.O.)

The mail has come today, and a friend writes
this to me: "The Masai have reported to the
district commissioner at Ngong that many times,
at sunrise and sunset, they have seen lions on
Finch Hatton's grave. A lion and a lioness have
come there, and stood, or lain, on the grave for
a long time. After you went away, the ground
round the grave was leveled out into a sort of
terrace. I suppose that the level place makes a
good site for the lions. From there, they can
have a view over the plain, and the cattle and
game on it." Denys will like that: I must remember to tell him.

The lion stands looking over the valley. Now, INTO FRAME: a
lioness . . . strolling slowly toward him.

PULL AWAY.

NOTES TO
THE SHOOTING
SCRIPT

1. In postproduction this was changed to: "He even took the gramophone on safari . . . three rifles, supplies for a month . . . and Mozart". As first written—"He was an animal who loved Mozart"—seemed a bit "purple" for the first line heard in the film.

2. This section was rewritten to change the focus from the idea that she "ought to have a hat," since it seemed obvious that someone of her intelligence would indeed have a hat when traveling in the sun.

3. This was rewritten as we staged it to eliminate the heavy colonial exposition and have Delamere tell a joke instead.

4. Again, we dropped the reference to her not wearing a hat.

5. Scene shot but eliminated during editing for length.

6. This was restaged during shooting to avoid giving the sense that violence was producing a kind of sexual arousal.

7. Scenes 48, 49, and 50a were rearranged in the editing process to create a better flow.

8–14. Scenes shot but eliminated during editing for length.

15. Scenes 65, 66, and 67 were all shot, but eliminated during the editing for length.

16. Scene 83a was shot as written, then trimmed to keep only the

155

African children and the cuckoo clock. The remainder was edited not only for length but for purposes of pacing—to get to the start of the war more quickly.

17. This scene was shot, then trimmed for length and pace. We took out the center section.

18. This speech was reduced during shooting to simply: "It was . . . fun." As written, it seemed preachy and too thought out.

19. This entire argument was lifted out during rehearsal just prior to shooting. It seemed to make a villain out of Bror and to make Denys seem pretentious and preachy.

20. The week before we shot this scene, it was rewritten into a much longer version that was filmed as follows: From Denys's speech as is to ". . . I mean, do they *know* they'll like Dickens?"

> KAREN
> You think they shouldn't read?

> DENYS
> I think you might have asked them.

> KAREN
> Did you ask to learn when you were a child? How can stories possibly harm them?

> DENYS
> They have their own stories . . . They're just not written down.

> KAREN
> What interest do you have in keeping them ignorant?

> DENYS
> They're not ignorant! I don't want them turned into a lot of little Englishmen.
> (then a smile)
> You like to change things, don't you?

> KAREN
> For the better, I hope. I'd like my Kikuyu to learn to read.

156

DENYS

My Kikuyu, *my* Limoges, *my* farm. There's an awful
lot to own, isn't there?

KAREN

I've paid a price for everything I own . . .

DENYS

. . . Oh? And what exactly is it that's yours?
(beat)
We're not owners here, Karen, we're just passing through.

KAREN

(a beat, then)
Is life really so damned simple for you, Finch Hatton?

And then Denys's answer per the script. This was changed for two
reasons. One: as first written, there seemed no real confrontation.
The argument seemed evasive and vague. Two: this seemed a per-
fect opportunity to speak directly to the armature of "possession,"
to entrench these people clearly on opposite sides of this thematic
argument.

21–22. For economic purposes I staged these angles as *interiors* rather
than *exteriors*. It saved about three-quarters of a night's shooting.

23. This was shot, then cut. It seemed misleading. Since we saw Karen
move away in the preceding scene, when we cut to Bror in the car,
we assumed that she was on her way and would discover him.

24. We never succeeded in getting this angle shot convincingly.

25. This scene was rewritten during shooting. I was afraid Karen's line
"I won't sleep with you" would get a bad laugh or that some realist
in the audience would shout: "Wanna bet?" Denys's speech "Life's
not years, Karen. It's just a day here, a minute there—a few fine
moments. You've got to collect them" seemed preachy.

26. This line was changed on the set to: "Why don't you get your
things?"

27. Shot but eliminated during editing for length.

28. This speech was taken out of this scene and inserted into scene

157

187/188 during rehearsal.

29. This scene was shot as written; then, during editing, I decided to play the first half voice-over (V.O.) a montage of traveling shots.

30. The speech from scene 180 (see note 28) was used, with revisions, in place of the opening as written of scene 187/188.

31. This speech was cut before shooting.

32. The four lines referring to the length of their stay were cut to keep the preoccupation of the scene purely sensual.

33. Shot and then cut.

34. This scene was shot and unfortunately had to be cut for length. It was beautifully played by Meryl and Malick, and I will put it back in when the film is sold to television, where length is not such a severe problem.

35–36. These scenes were rearranged in editing and put in later. (See note 40.)

37. Scene 208a was shortened to end with Denys's line "I did. She said yes," then moved to a late spot. (See note 50.)

38. This scene moved to a later spot and the first V.O. line was cut.

39. This scene was also moved to a later spot. (N.B.: All these changes, notes 35–39 inclusive, were done *after* shooting in the *editing* process.)

40. The new order as it exists in the released film goes from scene 201c directly to scene 214 (more information in note 50).

41–42. V.O. dropped.

43–48. All these scenes were cut before shooting.

49. This scene was shot, then cut during editing for length.

50. This scene was shot and cut for purposes of length. The new scene arrangement, then, *done in the editing process*, was as follows: From scene 201c to scene 214 (Berkeley dying) as indicated in

note 40.

Then directly to scene 216a (Denys asks Karen if he can move in with her).

Then to scene 217 as written in the script (Berkeley's funeral).

Then to scenes 218–223 as in the script (Denys moving in and the flying montage).

We then went from the end of the flying montage to the lovemaking scene described in the foreword, using Rascoe's dialogue.

Then *back* to scene 206 (see note 35) and played this section continuous through scene 207/208 and the *first part only* of 208a (as discussed in note 37). Then continuing through 209 and 210.

We then jumped *forward* to scene 255g.

These extensive rearrangements were made to clarify Denys's comings and goings, to try to eliminate what seemed a long, inactive section of the film, and to accelerate events in general.

51. Cut before shooting.

52–55. All scenes moved to a later position in editing. (See note 57.) The V.O. in scene 255m was cut.

56. This scene was not shot. The decision was made deep into the shooting when we knew we would have too much picture.

57. This scene (258) was inserted *after* scene 255g and *before* scene 255k. (See notes 52–55.)

58. Shot and cut for length.

59. There were major additions made to this scene the week we shot it. We tried to clarify thematic elements further and give Denys the opportunity to make one last defense for his kind of freedom. It was essential to put a large rupture in their relationship to prepare for their final breakup.

60. This scene was shot and unfortunately had to be edited out. It was another of my favorite scenes. The story point is made, however, in scene 260.

61. Cut before we shot.

62. This line was cut during rehearsal. Although it is a good line, I think the scene ends more strongly without the editorial comment.

63. Shot, then dropped for length.

64. V.O. edited to eliminate the reference to God, which seemed portentous.

65. During shooting, a visual reference was added here of Karen giving the dog to Juma. Then, at the end of Karen's V.O., a new scene was inserted as follows:

Kamante approaches Karen.

KAREN
You cannot come where I am going.

KAMANTE
There is no cooking where you are going?

KAREN
Well . . . you would not like it there. You must trust
me in this.

66. Dialogue referring to the dog was eliminated. (See note 65.)

67. The last two lines were eliminated while we rehearsed. They seemed less strong than Farah saying her name for the first time.

OUT OF AFRICA
Credits

A MIRAGE ENTERPRISES PRODUCTION
A SYDNEY POLLACK FILM

THE CAST

Karen	MERYL STREEP
Denys	ROBERT REDFORD
Bror	KLAUS MARIA BRANDAUER
Berkeley	MICHAEL KITCHEN
Farah	MALICK BOWENS
Kamanate	JOSEPH THIAKA
Kinanjui	STEPHEN KINYANJUI
Delamere	MICHAEL GOUGH
Felicity	SUZANNA HAMILTON
Lady Belfield	RACHEL KEMPSON
Lord Belfield	GRAHAM CROWDEN
Sir Joseph	LESLIE PHILLIPS
Belknap	SHANE RIMMER
Juma	MIKE BUGARA
Kanuthia	JOB SEDA
Ismail	MOHAMMED UMAR
Doctor	DONAL MCCANN
Banker	KENNETH MASON
First Commissioner	TRISTRAM JELLINEK
Second Commissioner	STEPHEN GRIMES
Lady Byrne	ANNABEL MAULE
Minister	BENNY YOUNG
Beefy Drunk	SBISH TRZEBINSKI
Rajiv	ALLAUDIN QURESHI
Young Officer	NIVEN BOYD
Mariammo	IMAN
Huge Man	PETER STRONG
Esa	ABDULLAH SUNADO
Victoria	AMANDA PARKIN

Lady Delamere .... MURIEL GROSS
Dowager .... ANN PALMER
Missionary Teacher .... KEITH PEARSON

THE PRODUCTION TEAM

Produced and Directed by .... SYDNEY POLLACK
Screenplay by ....KURT LUEDTKE
      Based upon the following: Out of Africa *and other writings*
      by Isak Dinesen, Isak Dinesen: The Life of a Storyteller
      by Judith Thurman, and Silence Will Speak *by Errol*
      Trzebinski
Coproducer ....TERRENCE CLEGG
Production Designed by .... STEPHEN GRIMES
Director of Photography .... DAVID WATKIN
Edited by .... FREDRIC STEINKAMP
                                WILLIAM STEINKAMP
                                PEMBROKE HERRING
                                SHELDON KAHN
Original Music Composed and Conducted by .... JOHN BARRY
Costumes Designed by .... MILENA CANONERO
Associate Producers .... JUDITH THURMAN
                                ANNA CATALDI
Executive Producer .... KIM JORGENSEN
Casting .... MARY SELWAY
First Assistant Director .... DAVID TOMBLIN
Production Manager .... GERRY LEVY
Camera Operator .... FREDDIE COOPER
Sound Mixer .... PETER HANDFORD
Second Unit Directors .... SIMON TREVOR
                                JACK COUFFER A.S.C.
Aerial Photography .... PETER ALLWORK
Location and Field Consultant .... JOHN SUTTON
Location Managers .... GRANIA O'SHANNON
                                ALLAN JAMES
Second Assistant Director .... ROY BUTTON
Assistant Directors .... GEORGE MENOE
                                PATRICK KINNEY
                                MEJA MWANGI
                                TOM MWANGI
Production Consultant .... MONTY RUBEN
Script Supervisors .... NIKKI CLAPP
                                LISSA RUBEN
Production Coordinator .... MARGARET ADAMS
Steadicam Operator .... STEVE ST. JOHN
Gaffer .... MAURICE GILLETT

Grips	RAY HALL
	IBRAHIM JIBRIL
	MAHMUD SHEIKH OMAR
	RICKY HALL
	ALI MATATA
	MOHAMED NGELA
	MOHAMED WAFULA
Best Boy	ALAN BARRY
Boom Operator	JOHN STEVENSON
Art Directors	HERBERT WESTBROOK
	COLIN GRIMES
	CLIFF ROBINSON
Set Decorator	JOSIE MACAVIN
Construction Manager	GEOFF LANGLEY
Prop Master	BERT HEARN
Assistant Costume Designer	JOANNA JOHNSTON
Wardrobe	KENNY CROUCH
	JENNIE HAWKINS
	ANDRES FERNANDEZ SOTILLOS
	STEPHEN CORNISH
	ELIZABETH RYRIE
	PAT MCEWAN
Costume Maker	DAVID GARRETT
Miss Streep's Hair and Makeup Artist	J. ROY HELLAND
Mr. Redford's Makeup Artist	GARY LIDDIARD
Chief Makeup Artist	MARY HILLMAN
Makeup Artist	NORMA HILL
Chief Hairdresser	VERA MITCHELL
Hairdresser	JOYCE JAMES
Postproduction Supervisor	ROBIN FORMAN
Associate Editor	CLAUDIO CUTRY
Assistant Editors	DON BROCHU
	JEFFREY BELL
	KARL STEINKAMP
	CRAIG HERRING
	SAUL SALADOW
	JOSEPH MOSCA
	RICK MEYER
Supervising Sound Editor	TOM MCCARTHY, JR.
Music Editor	CLIF KOHLWECK
ADR Editor	WILLIAM MANGER
Re-Recording Mixers	CHRIS JENKINS
	GARY ALEXANDER
	LARRY STENSVOLD
Music Scoring Mixer	DAN WALLIN
Local Casting (Kenya)	SARAH WITHEY
Production Accountant	BRIAN GIBBS
Publicist	PATRICIA JOHNSON

Stills Photographer .... FRANK CONNOR
Special Effects Supervisor .... DAVID HARRIS
Second Unit Camera Operator .... RODRIGO GUTIERREZ
Production Assistants .... DAVID HILTON
THOMAS THANANGADAN
Production Secretary .... CHRISTINE BUURI
Voice Casting .... BARBARA HARRIS
Chief Animal Trainer .... HUBERT WELLS
Kikuyu Advisor .... NELSON CHEGE
Music Research .... ALAN SMYTH
African Source Music .... GEORGE W. SENOGA-ZAKE

CONCERTO FOR CLARINET AND ORCHESTRA IN A (K. 622)
Written by WOLFGANG AMADEUS MOZART
Performed by JACK BRYMER, *Clarinet*
THE ACADEMY OF ST. MARTIN-IN-THE-FIELDS
Directed by NEVILLE MARRINER
Used Courtesy of PHILIPS CLASSICS PRODUCTIONS, THE NETHERLANDS

SONATA IN A MAJOR (K. 331) "RONDO ALLA TURCA"
Written by WOLFGANG AMADEUS MOZART
Performed by ANDRAS SCHIFF
Used Courtesy of LONDON RECORDS, A DIVISION OF POLYGRAM CLASSICS, INC.

SINFONIA CONCERTANTE IN E FLAT MAJOR FOR VIOLIN AND VIOLA (K. 364)
Written by WOLFGANG AMADEUS MOZART
Performed by ALAN LOVEDAY, *Violin*
STEPHEN SHINGLES, *Viola*
THE ACADEMY OF ST. MARTIN-IN-THE-FIELDS
Directed by NEVILLE MARRINER
Used Courtesy of LONDON RECORDS, A DIVISION OF POLYGRAM CLASSICS, INC.

THREE DIVERTIMENTI (K. 136, 137, 138)
Written by WOLFGANG AMADEUS MOZART
Performed by THE ACADEMY OF ST. MARTIN-IN-THE-FIELDS
Directed by NEVILLE MARRINER
Used Courtesy of LONDON RECORDS, A DIVISION OF POLYGRAM CLASSICS, INC.

Original Soundtrack Album Available on MCA RECORDS AND CASSETTES

Location Camps and Safari Transport Services Provided by
KER & DOWNEY SAFARIS, KENYA

Special Visual Effects by SYD DUTTON *and* BILL TAYLOR *of*
ILLUSION ARTS, INC.

Filmed in TECHNOVISION

164

Color by RANK FILM LABORATORIES
Prints by TECHNICOLOR

DOLBY STEREO *in Selected Theaters*

The Majority of This Motion Picture Was Photographed
on AGFA XT COLOR NEGATIVE

Main Title Design by PHILL NORMAN

Opticals by UNIVERSAL OPTICAL

Special Thanks to THE RUNGSTEDLUND FOUNDATION

RUNNING TIME: 150 MINUTES

MPAA RATING: PG

ACADEMY AWARD RECORD

BEST PICTURE	*OUT OF AFRICA*
BEST DIRECTOR	*Sydney Pollack*
BEST SCREENPLAY	*Kurt Luedtke*
BEST CINEMATOGRAPHY	*David Watkin*
BEST ORIGINAL SCORE	*John Barry*
BEST ART DIRECTION AND SET DECORATION	*Stephen Grimes* *Josie MacAvin*
BEST SOUND	*Chris Jenkins* *Gary Alexander* *Larry Stensvold* *Peter Handford (London)*

In addition, Out of Africa *received the following Academy Award nominations.*

BEST ACTRESS	*Meryl Streep*
BEST SUPPORTING ACTOR	*Klaus Maria Brandauer*
BEST COSTUME DESIGN	*Milena Canonero*
BEST FILM EDITING	*Fredric Steinkamp* *William Steinkamp* *Pembroke Herring* *Sheldon Kahn*

KURT LUEDTKE, 46, is a native of Michigan, a graduate of Brown University, and a former newspaperman who in 1979 left his position as executive editor of the Detroit *Free Press* to write screenplays. His first script, *Absence of Malice*, was nominated for an Academy Award and was produced and directed by Sydney Pollack. He is now writing a screenplay based on Thomas Keneally's *Schindler's List*. Luedtke continues to live in Michigan, where his wife, Eleanor, is vice-president of the Detroit Symphony Orchestra.

SYDNEY POLLACK, born in Lafayette, Indiana, in 1934, studied acting at Sanford Meisner's Neighborhood Playhouse in New York, where he also taught from 1954 to 1960. Working steadily as an actor during this period, he became friends with John Frankenheimer, then a television director, and went to Hollywood as dialogue coach on Frankenheimer's second feature, *The Young Savages*. Soon he was directing numerous TV shows, including episodes of *The Defenders*, *Naked City*, *Ben Casey*, and *Chrysler Theater*. He made his debut as a feature film director in 1965 with *The Slender Thread*, and his second film, *This Property Is Condemned*, was the first of six Pollack movies to star Robert Redford. His subsequent films include *The Scalphunters*, *Castle Keep*, *They Shoot Horses, Don't They?*, *Jeremiah Johnson*, *The Way We Were*, *Three Days of the Condor*, *The Yazuka*, *Bobby Deerfield*, *The Electric Horseman*, *Absence of Malice*, and *Tootsie* (in which he also appeared in the role of Dustin Hoffman's agent). He lives in Pacific Palisades, California, with his wife, Claire, and their three children.

FILM/THEATER/PERFORMING ARTS BOOKS
FROM NEWMARKET PRESS

MAKING TOOTSIE: *A Film Study with Dustin Hoffman and Sydney Pollack* by Susan Dworkin. The making of one of the biggest comedy hits of all time—"in a class with Lillian Ross's *Picture* and John Gregory Dunne's *The Studio* (Digby Diehl, *Los Angeles Herald Examiner*). 160 pp incl. 50 photos.

DOUBLE DE PALMA: *A Film Study with Brian De Palma* by Susan Dworkin. The only on-the-set study of Hollywood's master of the erotic-suspense thriller, while he made *Body Double*. "Film scholarship at its best" (Patricia Bosworth). 260 pp incl. 50 photos, filmography.

THE MELODY LINGERS ON: *The Great Songwriters and Their Movie Musicals* by Roy Hemming. The complete movie work of sixteen great composers in 400 pages, 162 photos, with filmographies, video listings, and full critiques. "Definitive, cheerfully gossipy, a must" (Clive Barnes).

THE BLACKSTONE BOOK OF MAGIC AND ILLUSION by Harry Blackstone, Jr. with Charles and Regina Reynolds. Foreword by Ray Bradbury. The legendary Blackstone story and history, science, and art of illusion from ancient to modern times. 248 pp., 250 photos, incl. 8 pp color.

AUDITIONING FOR THE MUSICAL THEATER by Fred Silver. Foreword by Charles Strous. Proven tactics and techniques by *Back Stage*'s "Audition Doctor" including 130 audition songs. "Authoritative" (*ALA Booklist*). 208 pp.

OUT OF AFRICA—THE SHOOTING SCRIPT by Kurt Luedtke. Introduced and Annotated by Sydney Pollack. The complete screenplay of the film that won 7 Academy Awards, including Best Screenplay, Best Director, and Best Picture. 192 pp. incl. 20 photos, notes, introduction.

Order from your local bookstore or write to:
Newmarket Press, 18 East 48th Street, New York, N.Y. 10017.

Please send me:
——copies of MAKING TOOTSIE @ $7.95 (trade paperback)
——copies of DOUBLE DE PALMA @ $8.95 (trade paperback)
——copies of THE MELODY LINGERS ON @ $29.95 (gift hardcover)
——copies of THE BLACKSTONE BOOK OF MAGIC AND ILLUSION @ $19.95 (gift hardcover)
——copies of AUDITIONING FOR THE MUSICAL THEATER @ $14.95 (gift hardcover)
——copies of OUT OF AFRICA—THE SHOOTING SCRIPT @ $16.95 (gift hardcover) and $8.95 (trade paperback)

For postage and handling, add $1.50 for the first book, plus $.75 for each additional book. Allow 2–3 weeks for delivery.

I enclose check or money order payable to Newmarket Press in the amount of $_____.

NAME _____

ADDRESS _____

CITY/STATE/ZIP _____

For quotes on quantity purchases, or for a copy of our catalog, please write or phone Newmarket Press, 18 East 48th Street, New York, N.Y. 10017. 1-212-832-3575.